THE BEST RECIPES FROM NEW YORK STATE INNS

THE BEST RECIPES
FROM
NEW YORK STATE
INNS

More than sixty inns from the
Niagara Frontier to New York City
share their traditional favorites
and house specialties.

YANKEE®BOOKS

A division of Yankee Publishing Incorporated
Dublin, New Hampshire

Compiled and edited by Georgia Orcutt
Designed by Alison Scott
Illustrated by Barbara Smullen
Yankee Publishing Incorporated
Dublin, New Hampshire
First Edition

Library of Congress Cataloging-in-Publication Data

The Best recipes from New York State inns.

    1. Cookery, American. 2. Cookery — New York (State) 3. Cookery, International. 4. Hotels, taverns, etc. — New York (State) — Directories.
I. Orcutt, Georgia.
TX715.B48567   1987   641.5973   86-51598
ISBN 0-89909-141-5

Acknowledgments

Special thanks to Bonnie Berrett, head of our recipe-testing program, and to the following people, who spent long hours cooking and evaluating the content of this book:

Chris Apitz	Stephen Kendall
Linda Bensinger	Donna and Paul Quinn
Deborah Bier	Peg Rodenheiser
William Farrier	Rich and Peggy Roth
Carla Kardt	Colleen Selmer

CONTENTS

INTRODUCTION

Most of us enter an inn through its front door. This book takes you around back and welcomes you at the kitchen doors of dozens of inns in New York State. If you choose to step inside and linger for a while, you'll find yourself at the very heart and soul of the inn business — its food. The recipes you'll find in these pages reflect dishes the inns and their regular clientele consider special — worthy of an evening out or suitable to serve a guest for breakfast.

We journeyed into the cooking world of New York inns to gather the best recipes chefs or innkeepers could share with us. We came face to face with a world far larger and more diverse than we could have imagined. In some cases, the culinary bests a chef proudly produced were traditional favorites. In spidery handwriting more than eighty years ago, Cora Krebs recorded a brownie recipe of her own invention; that recipe, from the Skaneateles landmark she founded, appears in this book, and those very same brownies are still baked at The Krebs each day from May through October.

On the other side of those eighty years, we talked with daring and innovative chefs whose favorite recipes bear the stamp of contemporary cuisine. With a twinkle in his eye, John Novi at the DePuy Canal House in High

Falls extolled the merits of his Day Lily Pesto. Anthony
Lynardakis at The Point in Saranac Lake explained just
how to make the tops of his individual Lobster Strudels
resemble flower petals.

We suspected when we set out, and confirmed along
the way, that there is no one style of cooking at New
York's inns. Although the state is united under one gov-
ernor and one mighty Thruway, it is, in fact, a vast and
far-reaching land of seven or eight separate regions. On a
trip from west to east, you can enjoy an early breakfast in
western New York, pause for a mid-morning snack in the
Finger Lakes, stop for a hearty lunch in central New
York, dip into the Catskills for late afternoon tea, make it
to the Hudson Valley or to New York City for dinner,
and push on to Long Island for a nightcap. It would be a
long, tiring, and filling day. And after driving more than
six hundred miles, you still wouldn't have set foot in the
state's largest wilderness, the Adirondacks.

In our travels and phone calls from one end of this
great state to the other, we've also rethought the defini-
tion of inn. You'll find a wide range of hostelries included
in these pages, from staunch, old-line hubs of activity
that have served their towns for generations to newcom-
ers that we felt were worthy of mention and that repre-
sent the regions in which they are located. Some offer
food and lodging; some only serve food. Our selection is
by no means comprehensive. We were disappointed to
learn that several fine chefs are currently at work on their
own cookbooks and could not share even one recipe with
us. And in several cases, when we discovered food we
couldn't resist, the chefs refused to put anything in writ-
ing because, they told us, they cook only from what is in
their heads.

As much as possible we've woven into our recipe
selection the "inside" comments and opinions of the
cooks. Henry-Paul at Le Chambord in Hopewell Junc-

tion reaches for Xeres vinegar when he makes a dressing for a duck salad, and we've told you that. Diane Lapidus at Gold Mountain Chalet in Spring Glen uses broth from cooking vegetables in her Tofu Mushroom Stew, and we've told you that. If you set out to duplicate a recipe, such things are important. But we must caution you about that very subject: In many cases, the larger inns prepare dishes in sizable quantities and use special short cuts that just don't make sense in a home kitchen. They also have a battery of machines and elves to stir, grind, chop, and peel. While every attempt has been made to adapt their recipes to what makes sense for you in your kitchen, there might be a few dishes that you can come close to but not duplicate exactly. We urge you to read the recipes, learn and understand the techniques and ingredients called for, visit the inns to find out more, and above all, get cooking.

BREAKFAST, BRUNCH & LUNCHEON DISHES

Ye Hare 'n Hounds Inn, Bemus Point, New York

GENESEE COUNTRY INN
Mumford, New York

PLEASANT VALLEY QUINCE JAM

In the 1800s the Indians referred to the area around the inn as Pleasant Valley, thus the name of this jam. Quinces are just about impossible to find in a store, but if you know someone who has a fruit-bearing tree, ask for some. This very hard fruit doesn't lend itself to many recipes. A food processor will be invaluable in preparing the fruit for cooking.

4½ cups peeled, cored, and finely chopped or ground quinces
3 cups water
1 box (1¾ ounces) Sure-Jell fruit pectin

½ cup lemon juice
1 teaspoon ginger
6½ cups sugar (or less to taste)

In a heavy kettle combine the quinces and water. Bring to a boil and cook, covered, for about 15 minutes or until the fruit is tender. Drain and return to the kettle. Stir in the pectin and mix well. Add the lemon juice and ginger, and cook, stirring constantly, over high heat until the mixture comes to a boil again. Add the sugar all at once and bring to a full rolling boil. Boil for 1 minute, stirring constantly. Remove from the heat. If foam has developed on the surface, skim it off and discard. Pour the jam into sterile jars and process in a hot-water bath for 10-15 minutes to seal. *Makes 4 pints.*

LANZA'S COUNTRY INN
Livingston Manor, New York

BLUEBERRY-RHUBARB JAM

If you or your neighbor has a rhubarb patch, you may be hard pressed to make use of an abundant crop. Don't overlook its possibilities in preserves. Rhubarb adds a pleasant tartness to this jam, and the blueberries provide color and texture.

2 ¼ cups blueberries
2 ¼ cups diced rhubarb
2 tablespoons lemon juice

7 cups sugar (or less to taste)
2 packages (1 ¾ ounces each) Certo fruit pectin

In a large kettle crush the blueberries, then add the rhubarb, lemon juice, and sugar. Bring the mixture to a rolling boil for 1 minute. Remove from heat, add the pectin, and stir well. Ladle the jam into sterile jars, seal, and process in a hot-water bath for 15 minutes.

Makes 4 ½ pints.

THE BAKERS
Stone Ridge, New York

GRANOLA

Purchase the following ingredients raw at a health food store and mix up as much or as little as you need, according to the ratio given below. (Use one cup, as we did, or any measurement of your choice to equal the specified "part.") The secret is in the long, slow cooking process, which releases natural sugars in the grains and sweetens the cereal so it needs no extra sugar. Store this hearty cereal in plastic bags; it will keep in the refrigerator for up to two months without losing its flavor or texture.

1 part raw peanuts	1 part rye flakes
1 part chopped almonds	1 part sunflower seeds
1 part cashew pieces	2 parts sesame seeds
2 parts rolled oats	1 part filberts
(oatmeal)	1 part currants or raisins
1 part wheat flakes	

In a large bowl combine all the ingredients except the currants or raisins. Pour the mixture into a large pan (a Dutch oven will work well) and roast, uncovered, in a 200°F. oven for 24 hours. Stir after the first few hours and occasionally throughout the cooking time. When the cereal becomes crunchy, remove from the oven, allow to cool completely, and stir in the raisins or currants.

Makes 12 cups.

THE WILLIAM SEWARD INN
Westfield, New York

MONTE CRISTO

This treat is especially tasty served the way the inn recommends — garnished with fresh apple slices and a sprig of parsley, plus hot maple syrup.

12 slices bread	12 slices smoked Swiss
Butter	cheese, cut to the size of
12 slices ham, about ¼	the bread
inch thick, cut to the	4 to 5 eggs, beaten
size of the bread	

Remove the crusts from the bread. Butter 1 side of 4 slices of bread and place 3 ham slices on top of each. Butter the top and bottom of 4 more slices and place 1 slice on top of each ham stack. Place 3 slices of cheese on top of each slice of bread. Then butter 1 side of the remaining 4 slices of bread and place 1 slice, buttered side down, on top of each cheese stack. Secure each sandwich with 4 toothpicks, 1 near each corner. Cut the sandwiches in half.

Melt 2 tablespoons of butter in a frying pan. Dip the sandwiches in the beaten egg, turning to make sure all the sides are well covered. Place the sandwiches in the frying pan, toothpick side up. Brown on all sides. (Push the toothpicks partway through to brown the top.)

Serves 4.

UJJALA'S
New Paltz, New York

WHOLE-WHEAT PANCAKES WITH FRESH FRUIT

Here's a wholesome, versatile batter that will keep for several days in the refrigerator. Ujjala Schwartz, who developed the recipe, also serves these pancakes sprinkled with shredded coconut and chopped almonds. White flour can be used to create a lighter batter, and chopped walnuts can be substituted for the sunflower seeds.

1 cup milk	1 tablespoon honey
1½ teaspoons white vinegar	1 egg
	Oil
1 cup whole-wheat flour	Sunflower seeds to taste
1 teaspoon baking soda	Fresh Fruit Topping
½ teaspoon salt	(recipe follows)

Combine the milk and vinegar and let sit until the milk curdles. Combine the flour, baking soda, salt, honey, and egg in a blender, add the curdled milk, and blend just until the ingredients are mixed. Heat a griddle or heavy skillet, grease the surface with oil, and spoon out the batter to make pancakes of the desired size. Sprinkle sunflower seeds on top of each pancake. Cook until bubbles form, then flip and cook on the other side. Use additional oil for each batch as necessary to keep the pancakes from sticking. Serve with Fresh Fruit Topping.

Serves 2.

FRESH FRUIT TOPPING

½ cup sour cream   1 teaspoon almond extract
2 teaspoons honey   Fresh fruit of your choice

Combine the sour cream, honey, and almond extract.
Top each pancake with fresh fruit, and top the fruit with
a dollop of the sour cream mixture.

MIRROR LAKE INN
Lake Placid, New York

ADIRONDACK FLAPJACKS

*These tasty, tender pancakes will be about ¼ inch thick
when cooked. Serve well buttered with warm maple syrup or,
for a change, with shaved maple sugar or whipped cream.
For further variation serve rolled around sausage links.*

4 egg yolks, beaten   2 cups flour
2 tablespoons sugar   2 teaspoons baking
½ teaspoon salt   powder
2 cups milk   4 egg whites, beaten until
6 tablespoons butter,   stiff
   melted

Beat together the egg yolks, sugar, salt, milk, melted
butter, flour, and baking powder. Fold in the egg whites.
Heat and grease a griddle and cook the flapjacks until
bubbles appear. Flip and cook the other side.   *Serves 4.*

MILLHOF INN
Stephentown, New York

STONE-GROUND WHEAT CAKES

These pancakes are delightfully light and flavorful and have been a Stephentown breakfast favorite for many years. Romana Tallet at the inn recommends Hodgson Mill brand wheat flour. For a variation add fresh blueberries after spooning the batter onto the griddle.

½ cup stone-ground wheat
  flour
1 cup white flour
½ teaspoon salt
3 ½ teaspoons baking
  powder

2 tablespoons sugar
1 egg
2 cups milk
2 tablespoons corn oil
Butter

In a large bowl combine the wheat and white flours, salt, baking powder, and sugar. In a smaller bowl mix together the egg, milk, and oil. Pour the wet ingredients into the dry and stir gently until they are mixed thoroughly; do not overmix. Heat a griddle and butter it well. Spoon the batter onto the hot griddle. Cook until bubbles appear, then flip and brown the other side of each pancake.   *Serves 4.*

BUTTERNUT INN
Chaffee, New York

BLUEBERRY BUTTERMILK PANCAKES

To make these refreshingly light pancakes, the inn recommends adding blueberries to the batter after it has been spooned onto the griddle. If you're in a hurry and don't mind a slight touch of blue throughout, add the berries along with the other ingredients. The inn always serves them with New York State maple syrup.

1½ cups flour	1 teaspoon vanilla
½ teaspoon salt	1 egg, separated
1¼ teaspoons baking soda	1 cup blueberries
2 cups buttermilk	

In a large bowl combine the flour, salt, and baking soda. Add the buttermilk, vanilla, and egg yolk and stir until barely mixed. Beat the egg white until stiff and fold into the batter. Drop batter by spoonfuls onto a hot, greased griddle. Add the blueberries and cook until bubbles form. Flip and brown the other side. *Serves 4.*

ROSE INN
Ithaca, New York

BLACK FOREST APPLE PANCAKES

Cut these large pancakes into wedges and serve with fresh fruit on the side and apple butter, jam, or syrup.

3 eggs	2 tablespoons margarine
½ cup milk	or butter-flavored
¾ cup Bisquick	Crisco
1 tablespoon sugar	1 large apple, peeled,
¼ teaspoon baking soda	quartered, and sliced
½ cup golden raisins	Cinnamon sugar to taste

In a blender combine the eggs, milk, Bisquick, sugar, and baking soda. Put the raisins in a bowl and pour the batter over them. Cover and refrigerate overnight. To cook, heat two 6- to 8-inch omelet pans until hot. Grease with margarine or Crisco and ladle one-quarter of the batter into each. (Try to ladle in as many raisins as possible for this bottom layer of the pancake.) Cover each with the apple slices and add the remaining batter. Cook over low heat for 15 minutes (the top layer will be runny). Place the pancakes under the broiler to firm up the top. Turn the pancakes and cook on the other side for 10 minutes. Place on dinner plates and sprinkle with cinnamon sugar.   *Serves 2.*

THE BAKERS
Stone Ridge, New York

DUTCH BABY

Doug and Linda Baker say this delightful popoverlike treat is the hands-down favorite of their guests. The dish takes its name from the caps Dutch babies wore during the Renaissance.

¼ cup butter	1 tablespoon cinnamon,
4 eggs	nutmeg, and mace
1 cup flour	(combined)
1 cup milk	1 teaspoon vanilla

Preheat oven to 400°F. Place the butter in a 5x7-inch loaf pan, then place the pan in the oven to melt the butter, making sure it doesn't burn. Place the eggs in a bowl and beat until just blended. Add the flour and milk and mix with a whisk until just blended. (Do not over-mix; batter should be slightly lumpy.) Add the cinnamon, nutmeg, mace, and vanilla and stir gently. Pour the batter into the loaf pan and return the pan to the oven. Bake 20-25 minutes or until puffy and brown. To serve, cut into quarters. *Serves 4.*

THE WILLIAM SEWARD INN
Westfield, New York

PUFF PANCAKES

One of the inn's best-loved breakfast recipes is this one for pancakes with a twist. Serve with powdered sugar and hot maple syrup, accompanied by sliced bananas, strawberries, or blueberries, and plump sausages.

6 eggs	1 cup milk
¾ teaspoon salt	¼ cup orange juice
½ cup sugar	3 tablespoons butter,
1 cup flour	melted

Preheat oven to 450°F. Beat together the eggs, salt, and sugar. Add the flour and beat again. Add the milk, orange juice, and butter and beat again. Pour about ½ cup of the batter into each of 8 well-greased 6-ounce ramekins. (The inn recommends spraying the ramekins with vegetable cooking spray.) Place in the oven on the center rack and bake 18-20 minutes or until puffy and lightly browned. *Serves 8.*

GENESEE COUNTRY INN
Mumford, New York

APPLE PUFF

Western New York State is noted for its many varieties of apples, which inspired this late breakfast or light dessert dish. Serve with bacon or toast as a special fall treat.

4 tablespoons butter
2 apples, peeled, cored, and thinly sliced
3 tablespoons granulated sugar
½ teaspoon grated lemon peel
3 eggs
1¼ cups milk
⅓ cup flour
1½ tablespoons granulated sugar
½ teaspoon vanilla
½ teaspoon nutmeg
¼ cup confectioners' sugar

Preheat oven to 425°F. Melt the butter in a skillet, then sauté the apple slices with the 3 tablespoons granulated sugar and lemon peel for about 5 minutes or until tender. Turn into a buttered, 9-inch square baking dish. Blend the eggs, milk, flour, 1½ tablespoons granulated sugar, vanilla, and nutmeg and pour mixture over the apples. Bake 10 minutes. Sift the confectioners' sugar over the top. Bake 10 minutes or until the puff is set and golden brown. Serve immediately. *Serves 4.*

THE BAKERS
Stone Ridge, New York

PILLOW PUFF
WITH FIG AND PEAR FILLING

For this recipe, the Bakers rely on a machine that separates the fruit pulp from the seeds. If you don't own such a machine, you can chop the fruit. The tasty topping also goes well with carrot cake.

1 package dry yeast	3 cups flour, sifted
¼ cup warm water	Fig and Pear Filling
⅓ cup butter	(recipe follows)
¼ cup sugar	1 egg white, slightly
1 teaspoon salt	beaten
½ cup milk, scalded	Cream Cheese Topping
2 eggs, beaten	(recipe follows)
1 teaspoon grated lemon	
zest	

Dissolve the yeast in the warm water and set aside to proof. Put the butter, sugar, and salt in a large bowl and pour in the scalded milk. Cool. Add the beaten eggs, lemon zest, and 1 cup of the flour. Beat well. Stir in the dissolved yeast and remaining flour. Cover and refrigerate overnight.

Prepare the Fig and Pear Filling. Preheat oven to 400°F. Working on a well-floured surface and keeping your hands and the rolling pin well floured, roll the dough out to ⅛ inch thick and cut into 4-inch squares. Put about 1 tablespoon of the filling in each square and fold the four corners into the center, pinching them together tightly to form a little "pillow." Place the pillows on a buttered cookie sheet and brush with the beaten egg white. Bake 10-12 minutes or until well browned. Remove from the oven and cool 10 minutes. Top each pillow with 1 teaspoon of Cream Cheese Topping.   *Makes 1 dozen.*

FIG AND PEAR FILLING

1 pound fresh, ripe pears   ¼ cup water
¼ pound fresh figs

Peel and core the pears. Remove the fig stems. Cut both into 1-inch chunks. In a medium saucepan combine the fruit and water. Cook, covered, over medium heat for 10 minutes, stirring once. Remove the cover and cook 15-20 minutes more until fruit is very soft. Purée in a food processor or blender. Cool thoroughly.

CREAM CHEESE TOPPING

1 package (3 ounces)   1½ tablespoons sugar
   cream cheese   ¾ teaspoon vanilla
1½ tablespoons butter,
   softened

Combine all the ingredients and beat until smooth.

THE ASTORIA
Rosendale, New York

FRENCH TOAST

French-born Jeannine Gleissner, who developed this recipe for "French" toast at her eight-bedroom inn, tells this story: "About seventeen years ago, I was asked to make French toast. French toast? At first I thought it must be a dish from somewhere around Normandy. (I am from the south of France — Provence.) Here is the version I developed, a dish that is French only in the imagination of the American people!"

Jeannine makes her own brioche from scratch (her recipe follows), but she recommends that readers find the nearest French bakery and buy day-old loaves.

1 loaf day-old brioche (recipe follows)	2 tablespoons sugar
	4 tablespoons butter
2 cups half-and-half	Orange slices for garnish
5 eggs, well beaten	Maple syrup, warmed
2 tablespoons vanilla	

Cut the bread into 1-inch-thick slices. Combine the half-and-half, beaten eggs, vanilla, and sugar. Beat until smooth. Arrange the bread slices in a single layer in a shallow dish or baking pan. Pour the egg mixture over them, poke the bread with a fork to help it soak up the liquid, and let it soak 5 minutes. In a large frying pan melt the butter over low heat. Arrange the soaked bread in the pan and cook slowly. Turn the slices after several minutes. Increase the heat to medium and brown the slices on both sides. Serve with orange slices and lots of warm maple syrup.   *Serves 6-8.*

BRIOCHE

A bread to glorify when it gets stale! Jeannine makes 4 or 5 loaves at a time. To get just the right texture for her French Toast, she freezes the loaves, then thaws them and stores them in the refrigerator for several days. Plan ahead to make this bread; it's an overnight affair.

Starter

2 packages dry yeast	½ cup (1 stick) sweet
⅓ cup warm water	butter, softened
¾ cup sifted flour	

Dissolve the yeast in the water. Add the flour and knead into a ball. It will be very sticky. Fill a large bowl with water (approximately 85°F.). Drop the ball into the water and make sure the water stays warm by adding more hot water if necessary. After a few minutes the ball will expand and float to the surface. Remove, pat dry, and put in a dry bowl. Add the butter and mix well. The finished starter will be very soft and wet.

Dough

4¼ cups sifted flour	½ cup (1 stick) sweet
3 tablespoons sugar	butter, softened
½ cup lukewarm milk	1 egg
(85°F.)	1 tablespoon heavy cream
1 tablespoon salt	
2 eggs plus 6 yolks, at	
room temperature	

In a large bowl sift the flour. Make a well in the center

(continued on next page)

(continued from preceding page)

and add the sugar, milk, salt, 2 eggs plus 6 yolks, and butter. Using one hand only, knead the dough into a wet, sticky ball. (Do not add any more flour; the dough will be very wet.) Continue kneading until the dough feels less sticky. Move the dough to a clean, dry surface. Pick it up and slam it down hard. Repeat this several times, alternating with more kneading, until the dough becomes springy and elastic (about 10 minutes).

Place the dough back in the bowl. Add the starter and work in well. Cover with a sheet of buttered waxed paper and a dish towel. Let rise in a warm place for 2 hours. Punch the dough down and refrigerate overnight. Punch the dough down again in the morning and turn into a large, buttered pan (the dough should take up about two-thirds of the pan). Let rise in a warm place until the dough doubles in size, approximately 2 hours. Preheat oven to 450°F. Make a glaze by beating the remaining egg and heavy cream together. Brush the dough's surface with the glaze and bake 45 minutes. If the top browns too quickly, cover it loosely with a piece of aluminum foil. Remove the bread immediately from the pan and cool.

Makes 1 large loaf.

GENESEE COUNTRY INN
Mumford, New York

GENESEE FRENCH TOAST

There's nothing ordinary about this version of an old favorite. In fact, it tastes like a cheese danish. The inn slices its bread into 1 ½-inch-thick slices, making about 12 pieces of toast from a loaf of French bread. To get 24 pieces, cut the bread into ¾-inch-thick slices.

4 eggs	12 slices day-old French
½ cup milk	bread, sliced on the
½ cup strawberry	diagonal
preserves	12 ounces whipped cream
½ teaspoon cinnamon	cheese, at room
1 to 2 tablespoons Grand	temperature
Marnier (optional)	4 to 6 tablespoons butter

Combine the eggs and milk in a flat bowl and beat until blended. Set aside. In a small saucepan combine the preserves, cinnamon, and Grand Marnier and heat thoroughly. Make 6 or 12 sandwiches, using 2 slices of bread and whipped cream cheese for each. Dip the sandwiches into the egg mixture. Melt the butter in a nonstick frying pan and cook over medium heat until brown. Remove to a plate and spread liberally with the warm preserve mixture. *Serves 6.*

THE 1770 HOUSE
East Hampton, New York

CRÊPES FLORENTINE

This light dish with a tasty filling can be sprinkled with cheese before baking or, for a more elegant brunch or buffet entrée, enhanced with a Mornay sauce.

4 eggs	1¼ cups milk
1 cup sifted flour	(approximately)
Salt	Florentine Filling and
3 tablespoons butter,	Mornay Sauce (recipes
melted	follow)

Combine the eggs, flour, salt, butter, and milk and blend until the mixture is the consistency of light cream. Heat a crêpe pan or a 9-inch frying pan until a drop of water sizzles on the surface. Lightly butter the hot pan and spoon in approximately 1 tablespoon of batter. Rotate the pan to spread the batter evenly. When the edges start to brown, turn and cook the other side. Remove the crêpe with a spatula and place on a warm plate. Repeat the above cooking method until all the batter is used.

Prepare the Florentine Filling and Mornay Sauce. Preheat oven to 350°F. Spoon approximately 2 tablespoons of the filling into the center of each crêpe and roll up. Arrange the crêpes in a shallow baking dish and cover with the sauce. Bake 15 minutes, then brown under the broiler.   *Serves 4-6.*

FLORENTINE FILLING

1 cup ricotta cheese
½ cup grated mozzarella
   cheese
⅓ cup grated Parmesan
   cheese
Salt and pepper to taste

Freshly grated nutmeg to
   taste
1 egg
1 package (10 ounces)
   chopped spinach,
   cooked and drained

In a medium bowl combine all the ingredients. Taste
for seasoning.

MORNAY SAUCE

2 ½ cups milk
1 slice onion
6 peppercorns
1 bay leaf
3 tablespoons butter

3 tablespoons flour
½ cup grated Parmesan
   cheese
Salt and pepper to taste

In a medium saucepan combine the milk, onion, peppercorns, and bay leaf and heat until almost boiling.
Remove from heat, cover, and let sit for 7 minutes.
Strain. Melt the butter in a clean pan, sprinkle in the
flour, and cook, stirring constantly, for several minutes.
Slowly add the milk mixture and cook over low heat,
stirring constantly, until thick. Remove from heat, stir in
the cheese, and season with salt and pepper.

THE BAKERS
Stone Ridge, New York

CRÊPES À LA COLETTE

These rich, buttery crêpes are very easy to make. Prepare the batter a day or two in advance so they will be ready to cook for company. Serve with butter and maple syrup or make them into a main course with a chicken or meat filling. If you don't own a bona fide crêpe pan, a 6- or 7-inch skillet will suffice.

1¼ cups all-purpose flour	½ teaspoon salt
3 eggs	6 tablespoons butter,
1 cup milk	melted
¼ cup water	1 teaspoon oil

Combine the flour, eggs, milk, water, salt, and 3 tablespoons of the melted butter in a blender and blend at high speed for a few seconds. Turn off the machine, scrape down the sides, and blend again for approximately 40 seconds. Refrigerate the batter in the blender jar or in a bowl 1-2 hours.

Heat a crêpe pan or skillet over high heat until a drop of water sizzles on the surface. Combine the remaining 3 tablespoons butter with the oil. Using a pastry brush, lightly grease the bottom and sides of the hot pan. With a small ladle pour 2 tablespoons of batter into the pan. If the batter seems too thick, dilute it with a few drops of water. Immediately tip and turn the pan so the batter quickly covers the entire bottom. (The crêpe should begin to firm up immediately; if it doesn't, your pan probably isn't hot enough.) Cook for approximately 1 minute; turn the crêpe with a spatula and cook the other side for another minute. Slide the crêpe onto a warmed pan. Grease the hot pan for each successive crêpe.   *Serves 6.*

ROUNDUP RANCH
Downsville, New York

JACKIE HOUCK'S BREAD PUDDING

Here's another way to make bread pudding. To keep the custard from drying out, place the baking dish in a roasting pan half-filled with water. Serve warm with maple syrup or whipped cream.

12 slices bread	12 eggs, beaten
Softened butter	2½ cups sugar
2½ quarts milk	Grated nutmeg to taste
1 teaspoon salt	

Preheat oven to 350°F. Spread the bread with butter and cut each slice into 1-inch squares. Place in a bowl and add the milk, salt, beaten eggs, and sugar. Stir gently. Pour the mixture into a buttered 8x12-inch baking pan. Sprinkle with the nutmeg. Bake 45-50 minutes or until a knife inserted in the middle comes out clean.   *Serves 8.*

THE 1770 HOUSE
East Hampton, New York

BREAD PUDDING

This version of the French dish Pain Perdu "always gets the guests down early for breakfast," report innkeepers at The 1770 House. Be sure to use a firm-textured bread; soft white bread will turn to mush.

3 cups cubed stale bread (preferably French brioche or babka)	½ cup sugar
	2½ cups milk
	1 teaspoon vanilla
½ cup white raisins	½ teaspoon cinnamon
½ cup (1 stick) butter, melted	Pinch of freshly grated nutmeg
3 eggs plus 1 yolk	

Preheat oven to 375°F. Butter a 9x5-inch loaf pan or a 1-quart baking dish and fill it with the bread and raisins. Drizzle with the melted butter. In a bowl beat the eggs plus yolk. Add the sugar and beat. Combine the milk and vanilla and slowly add to the egg mixture. Stir until smooth. Pour evenly over the bread and raisins. Sprinkle with the cinnamon and nutmeg. Bake 50-60 minutes or until the custard is set. *Serves 6.*

THE BAKERS
Stone Ridge, New York

FRITTATA À LA BAKER

A new approach to the Western omelet. For variety and color add red and green peppers, ham, or crumbled bacon. Use a heavy 8-inch cast-iron skillet or a pan that can go from stove top to oven. Allow 2 eggs per person and increase the other ingredients as necessary. Cut the frittata into wedges before serving.

2 tablespoons butter	1 tablespoon cream
½ medium onion, chopped	Salt and pepper to taste
6 to 8 thin slices zucchini	½ cup grated sharp cheddar cheese
2 eggs	

Preheat oven to 425°F. Melt the butter in a small skillet and sauté the onion and zucchini until soft but not brown. Beat together the eggs, cream, and salt and pepper to taste. Pour the eggs into the skillet and cook over medium heat until the bottom is set. (The top will still be runny.) Sprinkle the cheese on top of the eggs. Place the pan in the oven and cook approximately 15 minutes or until the top is puffed and brown. Loosen with a spatula and serve on a warm plate.   *Serves 2-3.*

UJJALA'S
New Paltz, New York

SHIRRED EGGS WITH VEGETABLES

Are you tired of eggs that are fried, scrambled, or poached? Here's a novel way to cook them. Chef Ujjala Schwartz presents this dish topped with her delicious sauce and surrounded by alfalfa sprouts so it resembles a nest.

2 tablespoons butter	¼ cup bread crumbs
¼ cup chopped mushrooms	Grated cheese to taste
¼ cup chopped zucchini	6 eggs
¼ cup chopped red pepper	Ujjala's Sauce (recipe follows)
2 tablespoons chopped red onion	Black olive or pimiento for garnish
1 tablespoon chopped fresh herbs (thyme, basil, oregano, and others)	

In a heavy skillet melt the butter and sauté the mushrooms, zucchini, red pepper, onion, and herbs until the onion is soft. Slowly stir in the bread crumbs until the mixture absorbs the liquid in the pan. Distribute the mixture evenly in the bottom of 6 buttered muffin tins or gratinée dishes. Add the grated cheese just to cover the mixture. Break one egg into each cup. Cover with more cheese. Bake 5-7 minutes until whites are hard but yolks are still soft. Before serving, top each with a dollop of Ujjala's Sauce and garnish with a slice of black olive or pimiento. *Serves 6.*

UJJALA'S SAUCE

½ to 1 cup sour cream
1 tablespoon Dijon
 mustard

1 teaspoon horseradish
Dash of garlic powder

Combine all the ingredients and stir until smooth.

COUNTRY ROAD LODGE
Warrensburg, New York

OATMEAL PLUS

Select your favorite oatmeal and cook as directed on the package, reducing the amount of salt specified in the instructions. To make the following hot cereal variation even more special, serve it with buttermilk instead of milk or cream.

For every 2 servings of oatmeal add:

¼ cup water
2 tablespoons raw bran
2 tablespoons wheat germ
Raisins to taste

Healthy dash of mace
 and/or pumpkin pie
 spice

THE CONCORD
Kiamesha Lake, New York

CHEESE BLINTZES

*A crunchy crêpelike wrapping around a rich cheese fill-
ing, somewhat reminiscent of cheesecake. Serve with a generous dollop of sour cream for breakfast, or top with strawberry
or blueberry sauce and serve as a dessert.*

3 eggs	3 tablespoons butter,
1 ½ cups milk	melted
1 cup flour	Butter or oil for cooking
3 tablespoons oil	Cheese Filling (recipe
Pinch of salt	follows)
2 tablespoons sugar	Fine sugar for dusting

In a medium bowl blend the eggs, milk, flour, oil, salt,
sugar, and melted butter. Mix well to form a smooth
batter. Heat a 6-inch skillet and grease well. Ladle in
enough batter to cover the bottom of the pan. Cook until
lightly browned and dry; lift out with a spatula and cool.
Grease the pan for each additional blintz. Prepare the
Cheese Filling. Place 1 tablespoon of the filling on the
browned side of the skin. Fold the edges over to form an
envelope. Fry in the butter or oil until nicely browned on
both sides. Serve hot, sprinkled with fine sugar.

Makes 16.

CHEESE FILLING

*You can substitute dry cottage cheese or pot cheese for
farmer cheese; ricotta can replace bakers cheese.*

1 cup cream cheese	1 egg
½ cup farmer cheese	1 teaspoon vanilla
½ cup bakers cheese	1 tablespoon sugar
1 ½ teaspoons flour	Orange and lemon zest to taste

Blend all the ingredients until smooth and creamy.

THE CONCORD
Kiamesha Lake, New York

QUICHE SUPREME

A breakfast or brunch treat for a crowd. Reduce the recipe as necessary for a smaller group; divide by four to make one quiche.

24 eggs	Pinch of nutmeg
1 quart heavy cream	2 cups shredded Swiss
1 quart half-and-half	cheese and smoked
4 tablespoons flour	Gruyère cheese
Pepper to taste	4 unbaked 9-inch pie shells

Preheat oven to 350°F. Combine the eggs, cream, half-and-half, flour, pepper, and nutmeg in a bowl and beat until smooth. Sprinkle the bottom of each unbaked pie shell with shredded cheese. Pour in the egg mixture. Bake 30-35 minutes or until firm and lightly browned.

Serves 24.

THE MERRILL MAGEE HOUSE
Warrensburg, New York

CHICKEN ALMOND QUICHE

A light and fluffy quiche, almost the consistency of a soufflé. The almonds create a fine surprise in texture. Bake in one 12-inch pan or use two 8-inch quiche pans. Cut into small portions, this dish also could be used as an appetizer.

½ medium onion, sliced
1 tablespoon butter
4 eggs
2 cups half-and-half
Pinch each of pepper,
   curry powder, and
   ground nutmeg
1 unbaked 12-inch pie
   shell

1 chicken breast,
   poached* and cubed (or
   approximately 2 cups
   cubed, cooked chicken)
3 ounces Swiss cheese,
   grated or cubed
2 tablespoons sliced
   almonds

Preheat oven to 350°F. Sauté the onion in butter until soft. Set aside. In a bowl beat the eggs, half-and-half, and seasonings and set aside. Arrange the sautéed onions on top of the pie shell. Layer in the chicken, Swiss cheese, and almonds. Pour the egg mixture over the layered ingredients. Bake 40 minutes or until the top is lightly browned and the custard is set. Let the quiche rest 10 minutes before serving. *Serves 8.*

*Poach the chicken in a liquid containing water to cover, 6 black peppercorns, 1 tablespoon chopped parsley, ½ teaspoon dried thyme, and 1 teaspoon salt.

THE ATHENAEUM
Chautauqua, New York

BROCCOLI LORRAINE

Broccoli forms the basis for this crustless egg dish. Cauliflower, or sautéed zucchini, onions, and peppers, or spinach also will work well.

1½ pounds fresh broccoli, thinly sliced, cooked, and well drained
3 slices bacon, cooked until crisp, drained, and crumbled
4 eggs

¾ teaspoon salt
⅛ teaspoon pepper
Pinch of ground nutmeg
½ teaspoon dry mustard
1½ cups light cream
3 tablespoons shredded Parmesan cheese

Preheat oven to 350°F. Place the cooked broccoli in a well-greased 2-quart shallow casserole dish. Sprinkle with the bacon. Beat together the remaining ingredients and pour over the broccoli. Place the casserole in a larger baking dish filled with hot water and bake 25-30 minutes or until set. *Serves 6.*

LINCKLAEN HOUSE
Cazenovia, New York

CHEESE SOUFFLÉ

"We find the weary traveler loves our cheese soufflé, which we serve with a little Canadian bacon, salad, and popovers," reports Helen Tobin at the Lincklaen House. Use yellow cheddar for the best color.

½ cup butter
½ cup flour
½ cup milk
⅛ teaspoon paprika

¾ teaspoon dry mustard
1½ cups grated sharp
   cheddar cheese
6 eggs, separated

Preheat oven to 400°F. Melt the butter in a medium-size saucepan. Blend in the flour and stir over low heat until smooth. Add the milk, paprika, and mustard. Bring to a boil, stirring constantly. Add the grated cheese and stir until the cheese is melted. Remove from the heat. Add the unbeaten egg yolks, one at a time, beating after each addition. Let cool to room temperature. Beat the egg whites until stiff and fold into the mixture. Pour into a greased 1½- to 2-quart soufflé dish or four 6-ounce ramekins. Put the soufflé in the oven, reduce the temperature to 375°F., and bake 30-35 minutes or until a knife inserted in the center comes out clean. *Serves 4.*

CAPTAIN SCHOONMAKER'S
High Falls, New York

CHEESE SOUFFLÉ FOR TWENTY-FOUR

Sam and Julia Krieg serve their soufflés, along with home-baked bread, sausage, and strudels, at a long wooden table surrounded by ladder-back chairs. This recipe is "contrary" to more traditional soufflé preparations, but the Kriegs say their beautiful, aromatic dish invariably evokes sighs of contentment all around the table.

42 extra-large eggs	1 teaspoon chopped fresh
1 teaspoon cream of tartar	dill
8 sprigs parsley, minced	1 teaspoon celery salt
3 to 4 scallion tops,	1 can (10¾ ounces) cheese
minced	soup

Preheat oven to 350°F. Separate the eggs into 3 large bowls — 2 for whites, 1 for yolks. Add ½ teaspoon of the cream of tartar to each bowl of whites and beat until stiff. Add the parsley, scallion tops, dill, celery salt, and cheese soup to the yolk bowl and beat until well blended. Divide the yolk mixture between the two bowls of whites and carefully fold in. Fill 4 well-greased, 1-quart soufflé dishes and bake 20 minutes. *Serves 20-24.*

THE ATHENAEUM
Chautauqua, New York

CRAB IMPERIAL

Serve this versatile dish in a baked pastry shell or over hot, cooked rice. To shorten the cooking time and eliminate the baking, continue heating the mixture in a saucepan after the crab has been added until it is thoroughly cooked.

3 tablespoons butter	¾ teaspoon Worcestershire
2 tablespoons minced	sauce (or less to taste)
green pepper	⅛ teaspoon paprika
2 tablespoons minced	⅛ teaspoon pepper
onion	1½ cups milk
¼ cup flour	2 tablespoons dry sherry
¾ teaspoon dry mustard	2 egg yolks
(or less to taste)	12 ounces crabmeat, fresh
¾ teaspoon salt	or frozen

Preheat oven to 350°F. In a saucepan melt the butter over medium heat and sauté the green pepper and onion until tender. Slowly stir in the flour, mustard, salt, Worcestershire sauce, paprika, and pepper. Add the milk and sherry and cook, stirring constantly, until the sauce thickens and comes to a boil. Beat the egg yolks and add a small amount of the hot mixture to the eggs. Return the egg mixture to the saucepan, stirring rapidly to prevent lumps from forming. Fold in the crabmeat and pour the mixture into a greased 1½-quart shallow casserole dish. Bake 25-30 minutes.   *Serves 6-8.*

MIRROR LAKE INN
Lake Placid, New York

CRABMEAT AU GRATIN

For those who love crabmeat, this dish is a delight. It can be served as an appetizer or a main dish held together by a minimum amount of sauce. To stretch it for additional servings, make about twice as much sauce and serve accompanied by noodles with herbs and butter and a tossed green salad.

2 tablespoons butter
1½ tablespoons flour
Pinch of salt
⅛ teaspoon dry mustard
1 cup milk
½ teaspoon Worcestershire sauce

¼ pound cheddar cheese, grated
4 cups crabmeat
¼ cup grated Parmesan cheese

Preheat oven to 300°F. In a saucepan combine the butter, flour, salt, mustard, milk, and Worcestershire sauce. Stir over low heat until the butter melts and the mixture is blended. Stir in the cheddar cheese and crabmeat and place the mixture in a 2-quart baking dish or into 6 scallop shells. Sprinkle the Parmesan cheese on top. Bake 10 minutes or until piping hot. *Serves 4-6.*

OLD DROVERS INN
Dover Plains, NY

BROWNED TURKEY HASH
WITH MUSTARD SAUCE

This recipe has been on the inn's menu since the Friday after Thanksgiving, 1955, when Beardsley Ruml, one of the guests, got together with the chef and developed a new way of using holiday leftovers. With a small skillet, you can make 4 individual portions. Be sure to chop the turkey and potatoes well, or the mixture will not hold together when cooked. For additional flavor, add a few tablespoons of finely chopped celery and a pinch of poultry seasoning.

4 tablespoons finely chopped onion	Salt and pepper to taste
1 tablespoon butter	2 tablespoons clarified butter
4 cups finely chopped cooked turkey (white and dark meat)	Paprika
	Chopped parsley for garnish
1 cup finely chopped boiled potatoes	Mustard Sauce (recipe follows)

Sauté the onion in 1 tablespoon butter until soft. In a bowl combine the turkey, potatoes, and sautéed onion. Season with the salt and pepper. Heat a 7-inch skillet until hot and grease generously with the clarified butter.

Sprinkle the hot skillet with paprika. (It will act as a browning agent as the hash cooks.) Add one-quarter of the hash mixture, packing it into the bottom and sides of the pan. Cover, reduce the heat to medium, and cook 5-7 minutes or until the edges are brown. Turn out onto a heated plate, with the crisp side facing up. Repeat for remaining portions. Sprinkle with chopped parsley and serve with Mustard Sauce.   *Serves 4.*

MUSTARD SAUCE

3 cups chicken stock	½ cup prepared mustard
½ cup beef consommé	2 tablespoons flour
2 tablespoons dry mustard	2 tablespoons butter

Combine the chicken stock, consommé, and dry and prepared mustards in a saucepan. Cook over medium heat, blending with a whisk until smooth. Combine the flour and butter to form a paste and stir into the mustard mixture. Continue cooking until the mixture reaches the consistency of heavy cream. Do not let it boil. Serve very hot, over the top of the hash or on the side.

BREADS

The Hedges, Blue Mountain Lake, New York

YEAST BREADS

LANZA'S COUNTRY INN
Livingston Manor, New York

REAL HOMEMADE BREAD

A quick and easy white bread. The recipe below will make 2 loaves. To make 8 loaves, increase the quantities by multiplying each ingredient by 4, but use only 3 packages of yeast. This bread also freezes well. Leave slices out overnight and use for delicious French toast.

1 package dry yeast	1 teaspoon salt
2 ½ cups warm water	4 tablespoons sugar
4 tablespoons shortening, softened	6 to 7 cups flour

In a mixing bowl dissolve the yeast in the water. Add the shortening, salt, sugar, and flour. Mix 2-3 minutes. Cover with a cloth and let rise until doubled in bulk. Punch down and turn out onto a floured board. Knead well, turning dough three or four times. Divide the dough into 2 equal portions (or into 6 pieces for smaller loaves). Place the dough in well-greased 9x5-inch loaf pans. Let rise until doubled in bulk. Preheat oven to 375°F. Bake 25-30 minutes or until loaves are brown and sound hollow when tapped. Turn out of pans and let cool. *Makes 2 loaves.*

Bread for a Crowd. The inn makes its bread in large quantities, baking 52 small loaves at a time. If you're faced with preparing a meal for a family reunion or other sizable get-together, follow the instructions above, using a number of bowls, and increase the quantities as follows:

½ cup plus 2 tablespoons
  yeast
¾ gallon warm water
1¼ cups shortening,
  softened

½ cup salt
1¼ cups sugar
35 to 36 cups flour

THREE VILLAGE INN
Stony Brook, New York

COLONIAL GRAIN BREAD

This is a very light rye bread. Brush the tops of the loaves with melted butter after baking for a softer crust. If you can't find pumpernickel and white rye flours, substitute 1 cup medium rye flour.

2 packages dry yeast	1 tablespoon brown sugar
6 tablespoons warm water	½ cup pumpernickel flour
2¼ teaspoons salt	½ cup white rye flour
1½ tablespoons lard	½ cup whole-wheat flour
1½ cups milk	4 to 5 cups white flour
3 tablespoons molasses	

Dissolve the yeast in warm water and set aside. Combine the salt, lard, and ¾ cup of the milk in a saucepan and heat until the lard melts. Set aside to cool slightly and add the yeast mixture. In a large mixing bowl combine the remaining milk, molasses, brown sugar, pumpernickel flour, rye flour, and whole-wheat flour. Add the melted lard, milk, and yeast and beat until smooth. (A mixer with a dough hook is ideal; use speed #2.) Add the white flour 1 cup at a time. Turn the dough out onto a floured board and knead about 10 minutes or until the dough is smooth and elastic. Shape the dough into a ball and place in a buttered bowl. Turn to coat well, cover, and put in a warm place until the dough is doubled in bulk. Punch down. Divide the dough in half, shape each half into a loaf, and place in 2 well-greased 9x5-inch loaf pans. Cover and let rise again until doubled in bulk. Preheat oven to 350°F. Bake 30-40 minutes or until loaves are brown and sound hollow when tapped. *Makes 2 loaves.*

HANSEN'S ADIRONDACK LODGE
Lake Pleasant, New York

LIGHT WHEAT BREAD

Makes lovely, large loaves, with slices too big to fit in a toaster. Great for hearty sandwiches.

2 cups warm water (105°–115°F.)	2¾ teaspoons salt
1 heaping tablespoon dry yeast	4 tablespoons butter
⅔ cup milk	6 to 8 cups white flour
¼ cup sugar	⅔ cup stone-ground wheat flour
	⅓ cup wheat germ

Place the warm water in a large bowl. Add the yeast, stir to dissolve, and let sit for several minutes. In a saucepan scald the milk. Stir in the sugar, salt, and butter. Let cool to lukewarm. Add the lukewarm milk mixture to the dissolved yeast and stir lightly. Add the flour and wheat germ and beat to form a smooth dough. Knead 10-12 minutes until the dough is smooth and elastic. Place the dough in a greased bowl and turn to coat well. Cover and let rise in a warm place about 1 hour, until doubled in bulk. Punch down the dough, turn it over, cover, and let rest 15 minutes. Divide into 2 equal pieces and roll into 9x14-inch rectangles. Shape into loaves and place each loaf in a greased 9x5-inch bread pan. Cover and let rise until doubled, about 1 hour. Preheat oven to 400°F. Bake approximately 30 minutes or until loaves are brown and sound hollow when tapped. Remove from oven, turn out of pans, and let cool on racks. *Makes 2 loaves.*

GARNET HILL
North River, New York

ORANGE RYE BREAD

A marvelously fragrant and flavorful bread, best served the day it is made. Once cool, slice any loaves you won't eat immediately and freeze; then take slices from the freezer as desired. Unfrozen bread that is more than a day old makes fine toast.

2 ¾ cups warm water	3 tablespoons grated
2 packages dry yeast	orange peel
½ cup firmly packed	⅓ cup dark molasses
brown sugar	3 ¾ cups rye flour
3 tablespoons butter or	5 ½ to 6 ½ cups unsifted
margarine, melted	white flour
4 teaspoons salt	

In a large bowl combine the warm water and yeast and stir until the yeast dissolves. Stir in the sugar, butter, salt, orange peel, molasses, and rye flour. Beat until thoroughly blended. Stir in enough white flour to make a stiff dough. Turn out onto a lightly floured board and knead until smooth and elastic, about 10-12 minutes. Place the dough in a greased bowl and turn to grease well. Cover and let rise in a warm, draft-free place for about 1 hour or until doubled in bulk.

Punch down the dough and divide it into thirds. Roll each third into a 9x14-inch rectangle. Shape into loaves. Place each loaf in a greased 9x5-inch loaf pan. Cover and let rise in a warm place until doubled, about 1 hour. Preheat oven to 375°F. Bake on the lowest rack in the oven about 40 minutes or until loaves are brown and sound hollow when tapped. Remove from the pans and cool on racks. *Makes 3 loaves.*

WINTER CLOVE INN
Round Top, New York

DILLY BREAD

A moist, tender bread with a fine texture and chewy crust. This bread tends to brown quickly as it bakes; watch it carefully and cover the top with foil if necessary.

1 package dry yeast	2 tablespoons sugar or
¼ cup warm water	honey
(approximately 115°F.)	1 teaspoon salt
2 tablespoons chopped	¼ teaspoon baking soda
onions	1 egg
1 tablespoon butter	2½ cups flour
1 cup cottage cheese	Melted butter
2 teaspoons dill seed	

Dissolve the yeast in the warm water and set aside to proof. Sauté the onion in the butter until tender. In a large bowl combine the cottage cheese, dill seed, sugar or honey, salt, baking soda, and egg. Stir until blended. Add the sautéed onion and dissolved yeast. Slowly add in enough flour to make a soft dough. Place the dough in a greased bowl, cover, and put in a warm place to rise until doubled in bulk, about 1 hour. Punch down the dough and knead on a lightly floured board until smooth and elastic. Place the dough in a greased 9x5-inch bread pan and shape into a loaf. Cover and let rise until doubled. Preheat oven to 375°F. Bake 35 to 40 minutes, or until the top is golden brown and the loaf sounds hollow when tapped. Brush with melted butter and let cool before slicing. *Makes 1 loaf.*

GREENVILLE ARMS
Greenville, New York

SOUR CREAM HERB BREAD

As this bread bakes, it gives off an aroma that is positively mouth-watering. The flavor is savory and slightly sweet, and a bonus is that it doesn't require kneading.

½ cup water	2 teaspoons salt
2 packages dry yeast	1 teaspoon marjoram
1 cup sour cream, at room temperature	1 teaspoon oregano
	1 teaspoon thyme
½ cup butter or margarine, softened	2 eggs, at room temperature
⅓ cup sugar	4 to 5 cups flour

In a large bowl combine the warm water and yeast and stir until the yeast dissolves. Let proof 5 minutes. Stir in the sour cream, butter, sugar, salt, herbs, and eggs. Beat in 3 cups of the flour until well blended. Stir in enough additional flour to form a soft dough. Cover and let rise in a warm place until doubled in bulk, about 1 hour. Punch down the dough and divide it into 2 portions. Place in 2 greased and floured 8½x4½-inch loaf pans. Cover and let rise in a warm place until doubled in bulk. Preheat oven to 375°F. Bake 35 minutes or until loaves are brown and sound hollow when tapped. Remove from the pans and let cool on wire racks.   *Makes 2 loaves.*

HANSEN'S ADIRONDACK LODGE
Lake Pleasant, New York

JULEKAKE

A lovely Scandinavian fruitcake type of bread.

2½ cups milk
4 packages dry yeast
6 to 8 cups flour
1 teaspoon salt
2 teaspoons cardamom
¾ cup butter
½ cup sugar
1 cup dried currants

1 cup golden raisins
½ cup red candied
  cherries
½ cup green candied
  cherries
½ cup candied citron
1 egg, beaten

In a saucepan heat the milk until lukewarm (not hot). Add the yeast and stir until dissolved. In a large bowl combine the flour, salt, cardamom, half the butter, and ¼ cup of the sugar. Add the milk and yeast to the flour mixture and stir until smooth. Let stand 20 minutes. Add the remaining butter and sugar. Mix well. Let stand, covered, another 20 minutes. Combine the fruit in a bowl and mix together. Stir into the dough and shape into 2 loaves. Place the loaves on a greased baking sheet or in 2 greased pie tins. Cover and let stand 15 minutes. Preheat oven to 350°F. Brush loaves with beaten egg and bake 45 minutes. *Makes 2 loaves.*

GENESEE COUNTRY INN
Mumford, New York

EASY SOURDOUGH CINNAMON ROLLS

Obtain starter from a gourmet food shop or make your own. These fragrant rolls are worth waiting 10 days for.

2⅛ cups self-rising flour	1 teaspoon grated orange
¾ cup Sourdough Starter	or lemon peel
(recipe follows)	2 teaspoons cinnamon
⅔ cup buttermilk	¼ cup butter, melted
½ cup sugar	Glaze (recipe follows)

In a mixing bowl combine the self-rising flour, Sourdough Starter, and buttermilk. (The starter and buttermilk should be at room temperature.) In a second bowl combine the sugar, orange or lemon peel, and cinnamon to form the topping. Turn the dough mixture out onto a floured surface and knead 15-20 times. Preheat oven to 450°F. Roll out the dough to form a 12-inch square and brush with the melted butter. Sprinkle the topping mixture over the dough. Roll the dough up like a jelly roll, seam side down. Cut it into twelve 1-inch-thick slices. Place the slices cut side down in a 9-inch square baking pan. Brush the tops with a bit of melted butter. Bake 20-25 minutes. While still warm, swirl the glaze on top of each roll. *Makes 1 dozen.*

SOURDOUGH STARTER
This magic ingredient improves with age and will last for years if it is properly maintained.

1 package dry yeast	2 cups unsifted flour
2 cups warm water	3 tablespoons sugar
(approximately 110°F.)	

In a 6-cup glass or plastic bowl dissolve the yeast in ½ cup of the warm water. Stir in the remaining water, flour, and sugar. Beat until smooth. Cover the bowl loosely with waxed paper and let the mixture stand at room temperature until it bubbles. This can take 5-10 days. Stir 2-3 times daily. The starter will develop a sour odor as it ferments. Refrigerate it after it ferments and keep it tightly covered. To maintain the starter, after using about ¾ cup, add 1 cup water and 1 cup flour to the remainder of the starter. Let it stand again at room temperature until it bubbles. Then cover as before and refrigerate. About once a month stir the dark liquid that accumulates at the top back down into the mixture. At room temperature freshen the starter with ½ cup water and ½ cup flour. Let the mixture bubble. Cover the bowl and return it to the refrigerator for storage.

GLAZE

1 cup sifted confectioners'	½ teaspoon vanilla
sugar	2 tablespoons milk

Combine all the ingredients and mix until they reach the consistency of very thin frosting. Add more milk if necessary.

BAYBERRY INN
Southampton, New York

BUTTER CURLS

These light, buttery rolls are good plain or rolled in cinnamon sugar. The recipe can be doubled easily; keep half the dough in the refrigerator while preparing and baking the other half. Extra rolls freeze well.

1 package dry yeast	3 to 3½ cups flour
¼ cup warm water	1 teaspoon salt
½ cup milk	Butter, softened
4 tablespoons butter	Butter, melted
2 eggs, slightly beaten	

Dissolve the yeast in the warm water and set aside to proof. In a saucepan combine the milk and the 4 tablespoons butter. Heat just until the butter melts. Let the mixture cool slightly to lukewarm and stir in the dissolved yeast. Add the beaten eggs, 2 cups of the flour, and the salt. Beat until smooth. (If you're using an electric mixer, blend at medium speed.) Stir in enough of the remaining flour to form a dough that can be kneaded. Knead until smooth. Refrigerate the dough for 1 hour.

Roll the dough out into a rectangle approximately ½ inch thick. Spread with softened butter. Fold the left side to the middle and the right side over to cover, forming 3 layers. Roll the dough out again to ½ inch thickness. Cut into strips approximately 6 inches long and ½ inch wide. Pour approximately 1 teaspoon of melted butter into each muffin tin cup (24 cups in all). Form each strip of dough into a spiral and place in a muffin cup. Put the tins in a warm place until the rolls are doubled in bulk. Preheat oven to 350°F. Bake 18-20 minutes or until golden.

Makes 2 dozen.

THE BENN CONGER INN
Groton, New York

IRISH WHOLE-WHEAT BREAD
WITH MOLASSES

A hearty, chewy bread, best served warm. Just what you'd
expect to find in a bread basket at a country inn. Unlike
more traditional yeast breads, this one calls for only one
rising.

¾ tablespoon dry yeast	2½ cups whole-wheat
1 teaspoon sugar	flour
2 cups warm water	2 teaspoons salt
2 cups white flour	½ cup molasses

In a large bowl combine the yeast, sugar, and ½ cup of
the warm water. Stir until the yeast dissolves and set
aside to proof. Combine the white flour, whole-wheat
flour, and salt in a dry mixing bowl and place in a warm
oven (170°F.) until the mixture is slightly warm. Add the
molasses to the dissolved yeast and let rest for 5 minutes.
Add the yeast mixture to the flour and slowly stir in
enough of the remaining warm water to make a sticky,
but not runny, dough. Place the dough in 2 greased
8½x4½-inch bread pans. Put in a warm place and let rise
until doubled in bulk, about 1 hour. Preheat oven to
350°F. Bake 30-40 minutes, or until loaves are brown and
sound hollow when tapped. Remove from the pans and
let cool on a rack before slicing.   *Makes 2 loaves.*

QUICK BREADS AND MUFFINS

THE BARK EATER
Keene, New York

IRISH SODA BREAD

A wonderful treat warm from the oven on a chilly winter morning, this bread is even easier to make than muffins. Serve soon after baking, as it does not keep well. If buttermilk isn't an ingredient you normally have on hand, purchase powdered buttermilk — wonderfully convenient and just as good as whole buttermilk.

3½ cups flour	Pinch of salt
¼ cup sugar	Raisins to taste
1½ teaspoons baking	1 cup buttermilk
powder	½ cup (1 stick) butter or
½ teaspoon baking soda	margarine, melted

Preheat oven to 375°F. In a mixing bowl combine the flour, sugar, baking powder, baking soda, salt, and raisins. Add the buttermilk and melted butter and stir to form a smooth dough. Mold the dough into a loaf on a greased baking sheet with edges. Bake 35-40 minutes.

Makes 1 loaf, or 6 servings.

THE HULBERT HOUSE
Boonville, New York

MARY'S DOUGHNUTS

For a special touch, shake some cinnamon sugar on top of these golden, mouth-watering doughnuts.

8 cups flour
1 teaspoon baking soda
1 tablespoon baking
   powder
1 teaspoon salt
1 teaspoon nutmeg
½ cup (1 stick) butter,
   softened

2 cups sugar
4 eggs
1 cup sour cream
½ to 1 cup buttermilk or
   sour milk
Oil for frying

In a large bowl sift together the flour, baking soda, baking powder, salt, and nutmeg. Cream together the butter and sugar. Beat in the eggs and sour cream. Stir in the dry ingredients. Slowly add the buttermilk, using only enough to form a soft dough. Knead slightly on a floured board. Roll the dough out to a ¾-inch thickness and cut into doughnut shapes with a cutter or with two juice glasses, one smaller than the other. Fry in hot oil at 350°F. for approximately 1½ minutes per side.

Makes 4 dozen.

THE HEDGES
Blue Mountain Lake, New York

BANANA BREAD

No mixer is needed for this quick bread. As with most other batter breads, it is important not to mix it too much! Add ½ cup chopped walnuts or raisins for additional flavor.

1 ¼ cups flour	½ cup shortening
¾ cup sugar	3 small, ripe bananas
½ teaspoon salt	2 eggs, beaten
1 teaspoon baking soda	

Preheat oven to 350°F. In a bowl sift together the flour, sugar, salt, and baking soda. Using a pastry blender or two knives, cut in the shortening until the mixture is crumbly. Mash or purée the bananas and add to the flour mixture along with the beaten eggs. Fold together quickly. Pour the batter into a greased 8½x4½-inch loaf pan and bake 45-60 minutes or until a toothpick inserted in the center comes out clean.   *Makes 1 loaf.*

THE INN AT COOPERSTOWN
Cooperstown, New York

COOPERSTOWN BANANA BREAD

Make 2 loaves using 8 ½ x 4 ½-inch bread pans or increase the baking time to 65 minutes and make one large 9x5-inch loaf. This is a favorite at the inn's Continental breakfast.

2 ½ cups flour
½ cup granulated sugar
½ cup packed brown sugar
1 ¼ cups mashed ripe bananas
1 cup chopped walnuts

3 ½ teaspoons baking powder
1 teaspoon salt
3 tablespoons oil
⅓ cup milk
1 egg

Preheat oven to 350°F. Combine all the ingredients and stir to form a smooth batter. Do not overmix. Pour the batter into 2 small (or 1 large) loaf pans. Bake 55-65 minutes or until done. Remove from the pans and cool thoroughly on wire racks before slicing. *Makes 1-2 loaves.*

BIG MOOSE INN
Eagle Bay, New York

ORANGE BREAD

This lovely, light bread makes delicious toast.

6 tablespoons butter or margarine	1 ½ teaspoons baking powder
1 ½ cups sugar	¼ teaspoon salt
2 eggs, beaten	½ cup milk
¼ teaspoon orange extract	Grated peel of 1 orange
¼ teaspoon vanilla	¼ teaspoon ground cloves
1 ½ cups plus 1 tablespoon flour	Orange Glaze (recipe follows)

Preheat oven to 350°F. Cream together the butter and sugar. Add the beaten eggs, orange extract, and vanilla. Beat well. In a separate bowl sift together the flour, baking powder, and salt. Add to the creamed mixture alternately with the milk to form a smooth batter. Stir in the orange peel and cloves. Pour the batter into a greased 8½x4½-inch loaf pan and bake 1 hour. Remove from the oven and pour the glaze over the top. Cool 15 minutes in the pan and remove. *Makes 1 loaf.*

ORANGE GLAZE

Juice of 1 orange	¼ cup sugar

In a small saucepan combine the juice and sugar. Heat just to a boil, stirring until the sugar dissolves.

THE BAKERS
Stone Ridge, New York

PEAR BREAD

The inn serves this creation warm, topped with butter and maple syrup.

½ cup whole-wheat flour	2 eggs
1 cup all-purpose flour	⅔ cup sugar
2 teaspoons baking	¼ cup milk
powder	1 tablespoon grated
½ teaspoon salt	orange peel
2 small, ripe pears (about	1 tablespoon unsalted
¾ pound)	butter, melted

Preheat oven to 375°F. Chill 12 brioche molds or a 12-cup muffin tin in the freezer. Sift the whole-wheat and all-purpose flours together with the baking powder and salt onto a sheet of waxed paper. Set aside. Peel and core the pears and cut into a fine dice. Set aside. In a large bowl beat the eggs and sugar until they are light and lemon colored. (Use a mixer at high speed.) With the mixer at low speed beat in the milk. Gradually stir in the sifted dry ingredients until the batter becomes smooth and creamy. Add the orange peel and diced pears and gently stir just enough to distribute them evenly throughout the batter. Remove the molds from the freezer and brush with the melted butter. Fill the molds with batter. Bake 30 minutes or until a toothpick inserted in the center comes out clean. *Makes 1 dozen.*

THE 1770 HOUSE
East Hampton, New York

LEMON TEA BREAD

Adjust the degree of tartness according to your own personal taste by increasing or reducing the amount of lemon peel and juice.

½ cup butter, at room temperature	1½ cups flour
	1 teaspoon baking powder
1 cup sugar	½ cup milk
2 eggs, beaten	½ cup chopped walnuts
Grated peel of 1 large lemon	Lemon Glaze (recipe follows)

Preheat oven to 375°F. Cream together the butter and sugar until light and fluffy. Stir in the beaten eggs and lemon peel. Sift together the flour and baking powder. Add to the egg mixture alternately with the milk. Fold in the nuts. Pour the batter into a greased and floured 9x5-inch loaf pan and bake 35-45 minutes or until golden brown and a toothpick inserted in the center comes out clean. Remove from the oven. While the bread is still in the pan, poke holes in the top with a fork or a thin skewer. Pour the glaze evenly over the top. Let the bread sit 10 minutes and remove from the pan.   *Makes 1 loaf.*

LEMON GLAZE

Grated peel and juice of 1 large lemon	½ cup sugar

Combine the peel, juice, and sugar and stir until well blended.

UNION HALL INN
Johnstown, New York

RHUBARB BREAD

A delightfully different quick bread. The sweet-tart combination is just right, making this a fine way to use an abundant rhubarb crop. Especially good for breakfast, brunch, or lunch, it also freezes well.

1 cup milk	1 teaspoon baking soda
1 tablespoon lemon juice	4 cups (1 pound) chopped
1½ cups firmly packed	rhubarb, dusted with
brown sugar	flour
⅔ cup oil	½ cup walnuts (optional)
2 eggs	½ cup granulated sugar
1 teaspoon vanilla	plus 2 teaspoons brown
2½ cups flour	sugar for topping
1 teaspoon salt	

Preheat oven to 325°F. Combine the milk and lemon juice in a small bowl. Let stand for 10 minutes. In another bowl combine the 1½ cups brown sugar, oil, eggs, and vanilla and beat together until smooth. In a third bowl sift together the flour, salt, and baking soda. Add the dry ingredients alternately with the milk and lemon to the sugar mixture, stirring until smooth. Fold in the rhubarb and walnuts. Divide the batter among three 8½x4½-inch greased and floured loaf pans. Combine the granulated sugar and 2 teaspoons brown sugar and sprinkle over the top of each loaf. Bake 45-60 minutes. *Makes 3 loaves.*

THE 1770 HOUSE
East Hampton, New York

ZUCCHINI-WALNUT BREAD

This is more than just another recipe for zucchini bread. Fewer spices are used in the batter, allowing the subtle zucchini flavor to come through. The golden raisins give it an appealing appearance as well as texture. The inn suggests serving it warm for breakfast with cream cheese that has a bit of grated orange peel mixed in.

4 eggs	¾ teaspoon baking
2 cups sugar	powder
1 cup oil	2 cups grated, unpeeled
3½ cups flour	zucchini
1½ teaspoons baking soda	2 teaspoons vanilla
1 teaspoon salt	1 cup golden raisins
1 teaspoon cinnamon	1 cup chopped walnuts

Preheat oven to 350°F. Beat together the eggs, sugar, and oil until very light and lemon colored. Mix together the flour, baking soda, salt, cinnamon, and baking powder. Add alternately to the egg mixture along with the zucchini. Add the vanilla, raisins, and nuts. Pour the batter into 2 greased and floured 8½x4½-inch loaf pans and spread evenly into the corners. Bake 60 minutes or until done.   *Makes 2 loaves.*

GREENVILLE ARMS
Greenville, New York

PUMPKIN BREAD

A hearty, stick-to-the-ribs quick bread, moist and quite spicy. Serve with cream cheese.

½ cup oil	1 teaspoon nutmeg
1 ½ cups sugar	1 teaspoon ground cloves
2 eggs	¾ teaspoon salt
1 cup puréed pumpkin	1 teaspoon baking soda
¼ teaspoon baking	1 ⅔ cups flour
powder	1 ½ cups chopped walnuts
1 teaspoon cinnamon	½ cup water

Preheat oven to 350°F. Mix together the oil and sugar. Add the eggs, one at a time, and beat until smooth. Stir in the pumpkin. Combine the baking powder, spices, salt, baking soda, and flour. Add the nuts to the dry ingredients. (This will prevent the nuts from sinking to the bottom of the loaf.) Stir the dry ingredients into the pumpkin mixture alternately with the water to form a smooth batter. Pour into a greased and floured 9x5-inch loaf pan. Bake 1-1½ hours or until a toothpick inserted in the center of the loaf comes out clean.   *Makes 1 loaf.*

UJJALA'S
New Paltz, New York

CHEDDAR CORNMEAL MUFFINS

For variety, add sunflower seeds and whole corn kernels to the batter along with the cheese. These muffins hold up especially well when buttered and reheated.

1 ½ cups whole-wheat flour	Pinch of pepper
½ cup cornmeal	1 cup milk
1 tablespoon baking powder	¼ cup butter, melted
½ teaspoon salt	1 egg
	1 ¼ cups coarsely grated sharp cheddar cheese

Preheat oven to 425°F. In a bowl combine the flour, cornmeal, baking powder, salt, and pepper. Beat the milk, butter, and egg and add to the dry ingredients. Stir until thoroughly moistened. Stir in 1 cup of the cheese and spoon the batter into greased muffin cups. Sprinkle the remaining cheese over each muffin and bake 15-20 minutes. *Makes 1 dozen.*

ASA RANSOM HOUSE
Clarence, New York

APPLE-RAISIN MUFFINS

Serve warm, with cream cheese or apple butter.

1½ cups unbleached flour
1½ cups whole-wheat
　flour
1 tablespoon baking
　powder
1 teaspoon cinnamon
½ teaspoon nutmeg

2 eggs
¾ cup sugar
½ cup oil
½ cup milk
2 cups chunky applesauce
1 cup raisins

Preheat oven to 350°F. In a medium bowl sift the flours, baking powder, cinnamon, and nutmeg. In a separate bowl beat the eggs and sugar until foamy. Add the oil and milk and mix well. Slowly stir the dry ingredients into the wet, mixing only enough to dampen the flour. Add the applesauce and raisins. Pour into greased muffin cups. Bake 18-20 minutes.　　　*Makes 1½ dozen.*

HANSEN'S ADIRONDACK LODGE
Lake Pleasant, New York

BLUEBERRY MUFFINS

The recipe for these wonderfully large muffins proves you can ignore the often-quoted warning to fill muffin tins only two-thirds full. Grease the top of the muffin tin as well as the cups so the batter won't stick when it rises over the top.

2 eggs	4 teaspoons baking
1 cup milk	powder
½ cup oil	1½ cups fresh or frozen
3 cups flour	blueberries
1 teaspoon salt	

Preheat oven to 400°F. Beat the eggs and stir in the milk and oil. Combine the flour, salt, and baking powder in a bowl and stir into the egg mixture until it is barely moistened. Add the blueberries, stir gently, and spoon the batter into greased muffin cups. Bake 25 minutes.

Makes 1 dozen.

Variations. If you like apple muffins, chop an apple and add it to the batter in place of the blueberries. Chocolate chips also can be added. Plain muffins can be enhanced by topping them with cinnamon sugar and chopped walnuts, sprinkled on just before baking.

BAYBERRY INN
Southampton, New York

BAYBERRY BLUEBERRY MUFFINS

Orange juice and molasses make these muffins just a little different.

1 egg	1 tablespoon baking
½ cup milk	powder
½ cup orange juice	½ teaspoon salt
¼ cup butter or	Pinch of nutmeg
margarine, melted	1 ½ cups fresh blueberries
2 cups flour	Molasses Topping (recipe
½ cup sugar	follows)

Preheat oven to 350°F. In a large bowl combine the egg, milk, orange juice, and butter. In a second bowl combine the flour, sugar, baking powder, salt, and nutmeg. Add the dry ingredients to the wet ingredients and fold together gently, adding the blueberries after the first few strokes. (Mix only enough to moisten the flour.) Fill 12 greased muffin cups two-thirds full. Prepare the Molasses Topping, sprinkle it on the batter, and press it in gently. Bake 20 minutes. *Makes 1 dozen.*

MOLASSES TOPPING

¼ cup butter	2 tablespoons molasses
⅓ cup sugar	⅓ cup flour

Mix all the ingredients until crumbly.

THE POINT
Saranac Lake, New York

OLD-FASHIONED ADIRONDACK
BLUEBERRY MUFFINS

The cooks at this inn have come up with a fine way to fill muffin pans: They use an ice cream scoop to spoon out the batter for these substantial, not-too-sweet muffins.

¼ cup sugar
1 egg, beaten
¼ cup butter, melted
2 teaspoons baking
   powder

½ teaspoon salt
½ cup milk
1½ cups flour
1 cup blueberries, lightly
   coated with flour

Preheat oven to 400°F. In a large bowl mix together the sugar, beaten egg, melted butter, baking powder, salt, and milk. Stir in the flour and the floured blueberries until the ingredients are just mixed, being careful not to over-mix or to crush the berries. Fill greased muffin cups and bake 15 minutes. *Makes 9 muffins.*

BUTTERNUT INN
Chaffee, New York

LEMON MUFFINS

A good accompaniment for seafood salad.

2 cups flour
2 teaspoons baking powder
½ teaspoon salt
1 cup (2 sticks) butter or margarine, softened

1 cup sugar
4 eggs
6 tablespoons lemon juice
Grated peel of 1 lemon
2 tablespoons sugar mixed with cinnamon to taste

Preheat oven to 375°F. In a medium bowl combine the flour, baking powder, and salt and set aside. In a second bowl cream together the butter and 1 cup sugar. Add the eggs, lemon juice, and lemon peel and stir in the dry ingredients, mixing only enough to form a moist batter. Spoon the batter into muffin tins, sprinkle with the cinnamon sugar, and bake 15-20 minutes. *Makes 1 dozen.*

WINTER CLOVE INN
Round Top, New York

LEMON TEA MUFFINS

Use small tea muffin pans to make these tart, lemony muffins.

1 cup sifted flour	3 tablespoons lemon juice
1 teaspoon baking powder	1 teaspoon grated lemon
¼ teaspoon salt	peel
½ cup (1 stick) butter	2 tablespoons sugar
½ cup sugar	¼ teaspoon ground
2 eggs, separated	cinnamon

Preheat oven to 375°F. Sift together the flour, baking powder, and salt. Cream the butter and ½ cup sugar until light and fluffy. Beat the egg yolks until thick and lemon colored and blend well with the creamed mixture. Add the flour mixture alternately with the lemon juice. Do not overmix. Beat the egg whites until stiff peaks form. Carefully fold the whites and lemon peel into the batter. Fill greased muffin tins half full. Combine the 2 tablespoons sugar and cinnamon and sprinkle approximately ½ teaspoon of the mixture on top of each muffin. Bake for 15-20 minutes. Serve hot with butter. *Makes 1 dozen.*

APPETIZERS

Mirror Lake Inn, Lake Placid, New York

AUBERGE DES 4 SAISONS
Shandaken, New York

CHILIES EN ESCABÈCHE

Tim and Liliane Knab, the proprietors of the Auberge, spent 15 years in Mexico, where they developed a penchant for fiery dishes. This traditional Mexican way of preserving jalapeño and serrano peppers is served at the bar with corn chips, ranch-style beans, and a host of incendiary sauces. By mixing the jalapeños with Italian cherry tomatoes and small golden peppers, the inn serves a mix that is to just about everyone's taste. The types of peppers available depend on the season, but they should all be small for this recipe, since larger bell peppers simply do not cook up the same way. The dish requires a variety of colors and textures as well as various degrees of heat.

1 pound miscellaneous peppers, including at least ¼ pound jalapeños	1½ cups cider vinegar 4 tablespoons kosher salt Water
3 carrots	1 tablespoon black pepper
1 onion	½ teaspoon whole allspice
2 stalks celery	3 or 4 cloves
1 small head cauliflower, broken into florets	1 large bouquet garni (5 or 6 branches Mexican
¼ pound green beans	oregano, 5 or 6
2 medium yellow summer squash	branches thyme, and 4 bay leaves)
2 medium zucchini	1 small head garlic or 12
1 cup oil	cloves

Pierce all the peppers. Cut the remaining vegetables into bite-size pieces. Heat the oil in a large pan. Add the peppers, carrots, onion, and celery and cook 5 minutes at medium-high heat. Add the cauliflower. (Beware: The aroma might be very strong!) Add the vinegar, salt, and enough water to make about 2 quarts of liquid. Tie the spices, bouquet garni, and garlic (halved) in a cheesecloth bag and add to the liquid. Bring the liquid to a boil. Add the green beans, yellow squash, and zucchini. Remove from the heat and let cool. Refrigerate at least 2 days. Remove the cheesecloth bag before serving.   *Serves 12.*

HUFF HOUSE
Roscoe, New York

HOLIDAY CRAB DIP

Horseradish is an important ingredient in this dip, which is well suited to holiday entertaining. Garnish the serving bowl with parsley and serve with crackers. If you use frozen crabmeat, make sure it is well thawed and well drained.

1 package (8 ounces) cream cheese, softened	1 ½ tablespoons dried minced onion
⅓ cup mayonnaise	½ teaspoon salt
1 teaspoon prepared mustard with horseradish (or mix ¼ teaspoon horseradish with ¾ teaspoon spicy brown mustard)	1 tablespoon chopped fresh parsley
	Dash of garlic powder
	6 ounces crabmeat

Combine the cream cheese, mayonnaise, mustard, onion, and salt and blend until smooth. Fold in the parsley, garlic powder, and crabmeat. Mound into a serving dish and present with crackers.   *Makes 1 ¾ cups.*

GENESEE COUNTRY INN
Mumford, New York

BUFFALO-STYLE CHICKEN WINGS

The inn suggests 6 tablespoons of hot sauce for these wings. If you don't like very hot food, reduce the amount by about half. Serve the wings warm, accompanied by the inn's special Blue Cheese Dressing and celery sticks. The inn usually fries them in deep fat, but they can be baked at 350°F. for 45 minutes.

3 pounds chicken wings
Salt and pepper to taste
Oil for frying
¼ cup butter
6 tablespoons hot sauce
   (or less to taste)

1 tablespoon white
   vinegar
Blue Cheese Dressing
   (recipe follows)

Cut the tips off the wings (reserve them for soup). Rinse the wings, pat dry, and sprinkle with salt and pepper. Heat the oil (deep enough for frying) to 380°F. Fry the wings in small batches until they are crisp and golden. Drain on paper towels. Combine the butter, hot sauce, and vinegar in a large saucepan over medium heat, stirring, until very hot. Reduce heat to low, add the wings, and toss until well coated. Serve warm with Blue Cheese Dressing.   *Serves 12.*

BLUE CHEESE DRESSING

⅓ cup crumbled blue
   cheese
⅓ cup sour cream

⅔ cup mayonnaise
¼ teaspoon celery salt

Combine all the ingredients and stir until smooth. Refrigerate until ready to serve.

MIRROR LAKE INN
Lake Placid, New York

CHEESE CANAPÉS

Keep a jar of this tasty spread in the refrigerator for surprise guests. You can prepare it well in advance. The recipe makes enough to spread on about 5 dozen crackers.

¾ cup mayonnaise
½ cup grated Parmesan
   cheese
½ cup grated onion

Dash of Worcestershire
   sauce
Pinch of salt and pepper

Combine all the ingredients and mix until smooth. Spread on the party crackers of your choice, broil, and serve. *Makes 1½ cups.*

AUBERGE DES 4 SAISONS
Shandaken, New York

FOIE GRAS PROVENÇALE EN SALADE

Fresh foie gras is now being produced in upstate New York and is available from Iron Gate Products, 424 West 54th Street, New York City. It is recommended in this recipe, which neatly encases the foie gras in a crispy golden shell. Serve warm on a bed of greens.

1 small whole fresh foie gras
Flour seasoned with salt and pepper for dredging
1 egg, beaten
1 teaspoon chopped garlic
1 cup toasted bread crumbs
2 tablespoons clarified butter or olive oil
2 shallots, chopped
½ ounce dried or ¼ pound fresh cèpes
¼ pound button mushrooms

½ cup dry white wine
1 cup strong beef stock or 2 tablespoons meat glaze
Juice of 1 lemon or 2 tablespoons sherry vinegar
Salt and pepper to taste
3 kinds of salad greens (preferably Boston lettuce, escarole, red leaf lettuce, spinach, or nasturtium leaves with a few flowers)

Clean 1 small whole foie gras, removing any veins and nervous tissue that remain. Cut into 6 slices, each no more than ½ inch thick. (Use a wire cheese cutter and work with the foie gras when it is very cold.) Dredge the slices in the seasoned flour and then dip into the beaten egg. Mix the chopped garlic thoroughly with the bread crumbs and coat the slices of foie gras with them. Chill the slices for at least an hour so they will absorb the egg.

Heat the clarified butter or olive oil in a pan. (Clarified butter will give the slices a more golden color; olive oil is more authentic in this preparation, but don't use a fruity extra-virgin olive oil, as the taste is too strong. A golden-colored virgin oil such as James Plagniol is best.) Sauté the slices one or two at a time until golden on both sides, adding more oil or butter as needed. Set aside.

Add the shallots to the pan and cook 1-2 minutes. Add the cèpes and button mushrooms and toss for a minute or two. (If using dried cèpes, reserve the soaking liquid and add it to the stock.) Add the white wine and the stock or meat glaze and reduce over high heat until most of the liquid has evaporated. (This should form a thick emulsion.) Add the lemon juice or sherry vinegar and salt and pepper to taste, beating with a whisk until smooth. Return the slices of foie gras to the pan just long enough to reheat. Place each slice on a bed of greens, pour the sauce and mushrooms around each slice, and serve.

Serves 6.

DEPUY CANAL HOUSE
High Falls, New York

CONFIT OF DUCK BREAST WITH CATSKILL FOIE GRAS

This exciting dish can be prepared in advance, making it ideal as an appetizer or light luncheon treat. Make the confit itself from 1 week to 6 months ahead of time; it improves with age. Any type of duck can be used, but chef John Novi recommends mallard, since it has a fine flavor and texture. In this recipe the duck is served rare. Not fond of the canned foie gras commonly found in the United States, John uses fresh foie gras made by Howard Josephs in the Mongaup Valley of the Catskills. It is available from Iron Gate Products, 424 West 54th Street, in New York City, and comes in Grades A and B; for this recipe, Grade A is recommended. The garnish most commonly served with this dish at the inn is half of a poached onion cup filled with cranberry sauce, but fresh raw or al dente vegetables are superb as well, especially with a touch of lemon.

3 ducks (all the meat is prepared, but only the breasts are used in this dish)
½ cup white cooking wine
Fat trimmed from 3 ducks
24 leaves Belgian endive
6 slices Catskill foie gras, each 1½ inches thick

2 tablespoons clarified butter
6 Onion Cups (recipe follows), drained, and filled with 6 heaping tablespoons cranberry sauce

Cut up the ducks. (The breasts will be used for this dish; the legs with thighs attached, wings, and necks will be prepared in a confit for use in other dishes; the backs can be frozen for use in soups.) Remove the skin and fat from all the pieces except the breasts. Preheat oven to 300°F. Place the fat and skin, along with the legs, thighs, necks, and wings, in a roasting pan and bake at least 2 hours or until the fat is completely rendered.

While the other duck pieces are baking, trim the duck breast, removing the skin but leaving on as much fat as possible. Place the duck breasts, fat side down, in a very hot frying pan, with no oil added. Sear until the fat is dark brown; drain off at least half the fat. Add the drained fat to the roasting pan. Turn the duck and immediately add the white wine. Cook 5 minutes over high heat. Remove the breasts from the frying pan and place them in a crock. Add the liquid to the roasting pan.

When the fat in the oven is completely rendered, remove the other duck pieces from the roasting pan with a slotted spoon and arrange them in the crock. Strain the fat from the roasting pan. Pour the rendered duck fat over the top of the duck breasts. (If the recipe has been doubled or tripled, stack the duck breasts with fat between the layers.) It is essential that the top layer be completely covered with fat. Pour the remaining fat (or as much as needed) into the crock, again being sure to cover all the meat completely. Refrigerate for a minimum of 1 week.

To serve the confit, first prepare 6 appetizer or salad plates by arranging 4 leaves of Belgian endive in a fan shape on one side of each plate. Remove the desired number of duck breasts from the fat, carefully re-covering the remaining meat with fat. Wipe the meat and broil the

(continued on next page)

(continued from preceding page)

pieces, fat side up, for 5 minutes, until the excess fat has melted off and the meat is warmed through. (This meat should be served medium rare, but if it's too rare for your taste, broil for an additional minute.) As the duck broils, sauté the foie gras in the clarified butter, quickly browning it on each side. Slice the warmed duck breast. Where the endive leaves meet on the plate, place a slice of browned foie gras. On the other side of the foie gras, fan out 4 slices of the duck breast. Then place an onion cup filled with cranberry sauce on the side. Serve immediately.

Serves 6.

ONION CUPS

Peel 6 large round onions. Remove a slice from the bottom of each one so it will stand without tipping. Cut another slice from each top. Using a sharp knife, cut down into the body of each onion, loosening the flesh in a cone shape. With a sharp spoon carefully scoop out the flesh, leaving the sides and bottom of each onion intact. Blanch 4-5 minutes or steam for several minutes until tender.

LE CHAMBORD
Hopewell Junction, New York

ASSIETTE DIANE AUX GIROLLES

Refer to the Confit of Duck Breast recipe (page 86) for instructions on preparing the duck needed for this tantalizing dish. Chef Henry-Paul uses Xeres (sherry) vinegar, which has a strong, biting flavor. Red wine vinegar can be substituted. Chanterelles can be purchased canned, but for the best flavor buy them fresh and marinate them as explained below. Serve this appetizer with homemade rolls.

¼ pound chanterelles	Salt and pepper to taste
Marinade (recipe follows)	⅓ pound whole green
2 tablespoons Xeres	beans, boiled or steamed
vinegar	until tender
½ teaspoon Worcestershire	2 fresh artichoke bottoms,
sauce	cooked and sliced
1 teaspoon Dijon mustard	1 whole duck breast,
½ cup olive oil	prepared for confit,
2 tablespoons finely	thinly sliced
chopped walnuts	

Combine the chanterelles and marinade. Let sit for at least a week. In the center of two appetizer or salad plates place the marinated chanterelles. In a small bowl whisk the vinegar and Worcestershire sauce into the mustard. Add the olive oil, walnuts, and salt and pepper to taste. Whisk until smooth. Toss the green beans and artichoke bottoms in the dressing and arrange around the chanterelles. Add the duck slices to the plates. *Serves 2.*

MARINADE

¾ cup olive oil	1 clove garlic, minced
3 tablespoons Xeres or	1 shallot, minced
red wine vinegar	⅛ teaspoon salt
Pinch of tarragon	Pinch of pepper

Whisk together all the ingredients.

KITTLE HOUSE
Mount Kisco, New York

ESCARGOT EN CROUTE

A fine recipe for snail lovers. Use frozen, puff pastry shells to cut down on the preparation time.

7 large snails
1 clove garlic, diced
¼ cup sweet butter
¼ cup dry vermouth
½ tomato, diced
3 fresh basil leaves, diced
6 tablespoons heavy
  cream

Salt and pepper to taste
1 3x3-inch square puff
  pastry shell (prepared
  according to package
  instructions)

In a heavy saucepan sauté the snails in the garlic and butter. Add the vermouth, bring to a boil, and cook until the sauce is reduced by one-half. Add the tomato, basil, and cream and cook, stirring occasionally, until the sauce thickens. Season if necessary with salt and pepper to taste. While the sauce is thickening, heat the cooked pastry shell in a 350°F. oven 5-10 minutes. Spoon the snails into the center of the shell and pour the sauce over the top. Serve immediately. *Serves 1.*

ROSE INN
Ithaca, New York

SMOKED OYSTERS IN PUFF PASTRY

Succulent oysters in crispy shells. The red pepper dresses up this dish and adds a fine bit of color.

3 tablespoons chopped
   shallots
¾ cup white wine
1 tablespoon water
1 pint (2 cups) heavy
   cream
Garlic salt to taste
Lemon juice to taste
Tabasco to taste
¼ cup julienned sweet red
   pepper

3 cans (3½ ounces each)
   smoked oysters, well
   drained
6 patty shells (prepared
   according to package
   instructions)
Chopped fresh parsley and
   parsley sprigs for
   garnish

In a saucepan boil the shallots and wine until the wine is reduced to 1 tablespoon. Add the water and cream. Continue boiling the sauce until the cream has thick-ened enough to coat the back of a spoon. Season to taste with the garlic salt, lemon juice, and Tabasco. Add the red pepper and oysters and reheat just until the oysters are hot. Fill the patty shells with the oyster mixture, top with chopped parsley, and decorate with parsley sprigs.

Serves 6.

LE CHAMBORD
Hopewell Junction, New York

RISSOLES AU FOIE GRAS

A lovely, very special dish, easy to prepare and very tasty. Consult a recipe for puff pastry, or, to save time, buy a package of frozen, all natural puff pastry sheets and roll them out very thin. Executive chef Henry-Paul suggests serving this appetizer with sprigs of deep-fried parsley.

Puff pastry   1 egg yolk, beaten
12 ounces raw foie gras   Oil for deep frying
12 thin slices Virginia
  ham

Cut the puff pastry into 24 rectangles approximately 3 by 4 inches. Cut each rectangle into 2 triangles. Wrap approximately 1 ounce of foie gras in a thin slice of ham. Repeat with remaining foie gras and ham. Place the wrapped foie gras on 12 of the triangles. Brush the outer edges of each triangle with beaten egg yolk. Place the remaining 12 triangles on top of the wrapped foie gras and crimp the edges with a fork. Deep fry in hot (375°F.) oil, turning several times, until golden brown. *Serves 6.*

SHIP LANTERN INN
Milton, New York

COQUILLE SHRIMP

Could be served to 4 as a main dish.

½ cup tomato ketchup	½ cup mayonnaise
½ cup chili sauce	Pinch of fresh chopped
1 medium onion, finely	rosemary
chopped	Pinch of fresh chopped
½ teaspoon chopped	parsley
garlic	Salt and pepper to taste
½ teaspoon chopped	2 pounds (16 to 20)
shallots	Cooked Shrimp (recipe
3 tablespoons white wine	follows)
	Paprika for garnish

Preheat oven to 350°F. In a large bowl combine all the ingredients except the shrimp and paprika and whisk until smooth. If the sauce is very red, add a little heavy cream to give it a pink color. Arrange the cooked shrimp in a 1-quart casserole or in individual coquille shells. Cover with the sauce, sprinkle with paprika, and bake 10 minutes until hot and golden brown.   *Serves 8.*

COOKED SHRIMP

In a large kettle combine 1½-2 cups salted water, a few tablespoons of white wine, a few bay leaves, and a mirepoix (carrots, celery, onion, black peppercorns, and parsley stems, all finely chopped). Bring to a boil, add the shrimp, and cook 3 minutes or until tender. Remove the shrimp with a slotted spoon. Peel and clean.

THE 1770 HOUSE
East Hampton, New York

EGGPLANT ROLLATINE

This spicy dish makes a fine appetizer, or it can be used as a light meal or buffet item. As a variation, you can make small "sandwiches" by cutting the eggplants into disks, baking as directed, and then putting 1 tablespoon of cheese between 2 equal-size rounds of eggplant.

2 large eggplants
Salt
¼ cup olive oil
1 cup ricotta cheese
½ cup grated mozzarella
  cheese
¼ cup grated Parmesan
  cheese

1 tablespoon finely
  chopped fresh parsley
1 egg
Garlic Sauce (recipe
  follows)
Grated Parmesan

Cut the eggplants lengthwise into ¼-inch slices. Sprinkle with salt and let drain in a colander for about 1 hour.

Preheat oven to 400°F. Rinse the eggplant slices with cold water and pat dry. Arrange the slices on a well-greased baking sheet. Sprinkle with olive oil and bake 15 minutes or until brown. Set aside. Reduce oven temperature to 375°F.

Combine the cheeses, parsley, and egg to make the filling. Place 2 tablespoons of filling on each slice and roll lengthwise. Place in a baking dish and cover with Garlic Sauce. Sprinkle with additional Parmesan cheese and bake about 10 minutes or until heated through.

Makes 12 rolls or 24 "sandwiches."

GARLIC SAUCE

2 cloves garlic, chopped
¼ cup olive oil
2 cups canned plum
  tomatoes

½ teaspoon crushed red
  pepper flakes
1 teaspoon oregano
Salt to taste

In a saucepan brown the garlic in hot olive oil for 2 minutes. Add the tomatoes, pepper flakes, oregano, and salt and simmer 10 minutes.

AUBERGE DES 4 SAISONS
Shandaken, New York

CHAMPIGNONS À LA GRECQUE

Fresh white button mushrooms obtained from local grow-
ers are recommended for this light dish. Do not use any
mushrooms that have brown spots on them; the spots will
turn into ugly black blotches with this presentation. The inn
saves the stems to use for mushroom soup. Serve on a bed of
Boston lettuce. Once prepared, the mushrooms will keep for
up to a week in the refrigerator.

3 pounds white button
  mushrooms
4 lemons
1¼ cups olive oil
1 carrot, chopped
1 medium onion, chopped
1 stalk celery, chopped
1 tomato, peeled, seeded,
  and chopped (or
  substitute 1 to 2 canned
  whole tomatoes)
1½ tablespoons kosher
  salt
6 cloves garlic

2 tablespoons coriander
  seed
1 tablespoon fennel seed
1 teaspoon black pepper
1 teaspoon white pepper
Several grains allspice
2 cloves
1 bouquet garni (4 big
  branches good Greek
  oregano, several
  branches thyme, 3 or 4
  bay leaves, and 1 small
  branch rosemary)
Chicken stock or water

With a small paring knife remove the stems from the mushrooms, cutting them off flush with the caps and reserving them for another use. Do not wash the mushrooms until you are ready to pour the liquid over them. Squeeze the lemons and reserve the juice. (You should have between ¾ and 1 cup of juice.)

In ¼ cup of the olive oil sauté the carrot, onion, and celery until they begin to brown. Add the tomato and stir. Then add the lemon juice, salt, garlic, and seasonings. (Tie the spices and herbs in cheesecloth, or you'll be picking seeds out of your teeth for the rest of the meal!) Add enough chicken stock or water to make two quarts of liquid. (If you use water, season it with salt.) Add the remaining olive oil and bring the mixture to a boil. Pour the boiling liquid over the mushrooms in a pot and return to a boil. Remove from the heat and allow to cool. Refrigerate in a container with a drop lid to keep the mushrooms submerged for at least 24 hours before serving.   *Serves 6.*

THE POINT
Saranac Lake, New York

LOBSTER STRUDELS

Many people are intimidated by the delicate nature of filo dough, but this frozen packaged strudel dough has made elegant dishes such as this a reality for many cooks. Definitely impressive, these individual strudels are spectacular in taste and appearance, as they come out of the oven resembling flower petals.

1 pound lobster meat, cooked
1 bunch scallions, chopped
3 tablespoons chopped fresh dill
1 cup small curd cottage cheese
½ cup grated Swiss or Gruyère cheese

¾ cup sour cream
5 large eggs, beaten
Salt and pepper to taste
1 package frozen filo leaves (strudel dough)
Melted butter
2 to 3 lemons, cut into wedges

Preheat oven to 400°F. In a large bowl combine the lobster, scallions, dill, cottage cheese, Swiss or Gruyère cheese, sour cream, eggs, and salt and pepper to taste. Mix well. Butter 12 individual soufflé cups (4 ounces each). Use 1½ sheets of filo for each cup, laying them in evenly and being sure to cover the bottom of each. Fill each cup with a scant ½ cup of the mixture. Pull the corners of the filo together and twist gently to close the top without breaking the filo. Drizzle the top of the filo with melted butter. Bake 25 minutes. Serve with lemon wedges. *Serves 12.*

TROUTBECK
Amenia, New York

SHIITAKE SAUTÉ

Shiitake mushrooms have a wonderful, meaty consistency and mild flavor, quite unlike that of varieties commonly found in the supermarket. Many specialty stores sell them fresh. In a pinch, buy them dried and rehydrate them as directed on the package. This dish makes a fine first course for a very special occasion; or, serve as a side dish for 4 to 5 people.

1 pound shiitake mushrooms	2 minced shallots
¼ cup clarified butter	Pepper to taste
3 ounces Westphalian or Black Forest ham, cut into thin strips	¼ cup Madeira (or more to taste)

Trim the stems of the mushrooms close to the ground ends and slice them lengthwise into large pieces. Sauté them in the clarified butter. Add the ham and shallots and toss until evenly mixed. Season with pepper. Heat the Madeira slightly, pour over the mushroom mixture, and flame. Over high heat reduce the liquid by two-thirds and serve at once. *Serves 2.*

SOUPS & CHOWDERS

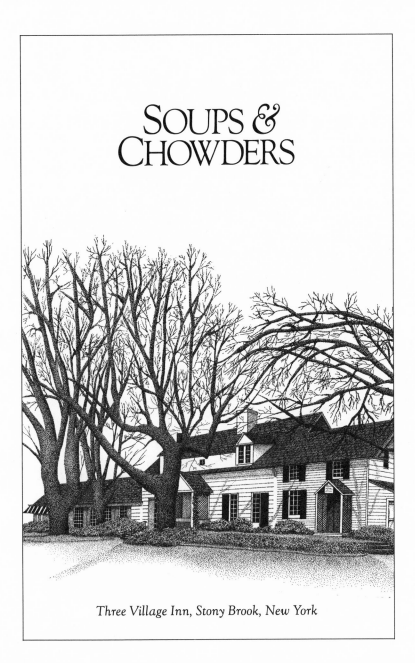

Three Village Inn, Stony Brook, New York

CHILLED SOUPS

GIDEON PUTNAM
Saratoga Springs, New York

GIDEON-STYLE GAZPACHO

The inn serves this easy cold soup garnished with bits of cooked shrimp.

3 ripe tomatoes, diced
1 can (8 ounces) whole
    tomatoes, drained and
    diced
1 green pepper, diced
1 large cucumber, diced
1 pimiento, diced
2 slices fresh white bread,
    cubed

1 clove garlic, minced
2 tablespoons vinegar
½ cup olive oil
Dash of Worcestershire
    sauce
Dash of Tabasco
Salt and pepper to taste
2 teaspoons paprika
2 cups V-8 juice

Combine all the ingredients in a large bowl and let stand overnight in the refrigerator. Purée in a blender or food processor and correct seasonings. *Serves 6-8.*

THE BIRD & BOTTLE INN
Garrison, New York

TOMATO AND DILL SOUP

A refreshing cold soup, slightly sweet with a strong dill flavor. It makes a fine first course as is. As an option, add ½ cup heavy cream while the soup simmers and serve as a luncheon entrée.

½ cup tomato juice
2 cups chicken stock
1¾ cups peeled, drained, and chopped tomatoes
¼ cup unsalted butter
¼ cup finely chopped onion
2 tablespoons finely chopped celery

2 tablespoons chopped fresh dill
¼ cup flour
1 tablespoon sugar
Salt and pepper to taste
Chopped fresh dill for garnish

In a medium saucepan combine the tomato juice, chicken stock, and chopped tomatoes. Bring to a boil, remove from heat, and set aside. In a second saucepan melt the butter over medium heat and sauté the onion and celery with the 2 tablespoons dill until tender. Stir in the flour and cook 5 minutes over low heat, stirring constantly, until well blended. Gradually add the soup mixture, stirring until smooth. Bring to a boil. Cover and simmer 15 minutes, stirring occasionally. Add the sugar and salt and pepper to taste. Pour the mixture into a large bowl. Cover and chill for at least 6 hours, preferably overnight. Ladle into chilled soup bowls and garnish with fresh dill. *Serves 4.*

MIRROR LAKE INN
Lake Placid, New York

CREAM OF CUCUMBER SOUP

Use care when heating this soup; if it gets too hot, the milk will curdle. Best served as a soup course for a large meal.

1 medium potato, peeled and chopped	1 medium onion, peeled and grated
1 cup chicken broth	2 tablespoons butter
1 cucumber, peeled and seeded	Finely chopped fresh parsley for garnish
2 cups milk	

Combine the potato, chicken broth, and cucumber in a blender and purée until smooth. Heat the milk, onion, and butter in a saucepan. Add the puréed mixture and cook over medium heat for approximately 20 minutes or until the potato is cooked. Serve hot, garnished with parsley. *Serves 4-6.*

GLEN IRIS INN
Castile, New York

CUCUMBER SOUP

Use a food processor or a blender to give this soup a smooth texture. If you want to make the soup thinner, add chicken stock along with the sour cream.

3 cups peeled, chopped, and seeded cucumbers
3 tablespoons olive oil
1 tablespoon dill seed
2 small cloves garlic, chopped

Salt and pepper to taste
1 cup plain yogurt
2 cups sour cream
½ cup finely chopped walnuts

Combine the cucumbers, olive oil, dill seed, and garlic and blend until smooth. Season to taste with salt and pepper. Pour the mixture into a bowl. Stir in the yogurt and sour cream. Chill. Spoon the soup into serving bowls and garnish with chopped walnuts.   *Serves 6.*

COUNTRY ROAD LODGE
Warrensburg, New York

CHILLED ZUCCHINI SOUP

A dollop of sour cream or yogurt sprinkled with chopped parsley or chives will set off the lovely, fresh green color of this easy-to-make soup. Serve for a summer lunch or as a first course at dinner.

3 tablespoons butter	1 tablespoon chopped
4 to 5 medium zucchini,	fresh basil or parsley or
chopped (about 4 cups)	1 teaspoon dried
2 cups turkey, chicken, or	Salt and pepper to taste
beef stock	Yogurt or sour cream

In a heavy saucepan melt the butter and sauté the zucchini until soft. Add the stock and the basil or parsley. Purée the mixture in a blender or food mill. Season with salt and pepper. Chill. Serve with yogurt or sour cream.

Serves 4-6.

UNION HALL INN
Johnstown, New York

COLD PEACH SOUP

A gorgeous, pastel orange soup — smooth, creamy, and thick. Serve as an appetizer or a dessert on a hot summer day, garnished with several peach slices or a sprig of fresh mint or lemon balm. Use the most flavorful peaches you can find; if you're faced with peaches that aren't perfectly ripe and juicy, reduce the amount of sour cream by about half.

5 large ripe peaches,   Juice of 2 lemons
  peeled and chopped   ¼ cup dry sherry
¼ cup sugar   2 tablespoons orange juice
1 cup sour cream

Purée the peaches in a food processor or blender. Pour into a bowl, combine with the remaining ingredients, and stir until well blended. (Or, if your food processor is large enough, add the remaining ingredients and blend until smooth.) Chill for at least 1 hour before serving.

Serves 8.

GIDEON PUTNAM
Saratoga Springs, New York

COLD MELON SOUP

A sweet, mildly spicy soup.

2 ripe cantaloupes or melons, peeled and diced
½ cup honey
1 cup orange juice concentrate
1 cup peach or apricot nectar

¼ teaspoon ginger
1 stick cinnamon
4 cloves
Pinch of allspice
½ cup heavy cream
½ cup plain yogurt
¼ cup melon liqueur
Mint sprigs for garnish

Combine the melon with the honey, orange juice concentrate, peach or apricot nectar, ginger, cinnamon, cloves, and allspice. Bring to a boil and cook 1 or 2 minutes. Cool and refrigerate overnight. Remove the cinnamon stick and cloves and pass the mixture through a blender or food processor. Add the cream, yogurt, and melon liqueur. Serve very cold, garnished with a sprig of mint. *Serves 8-10.*

THE ATHENAEUM
Chautauqua, New York

STRAWBERRY SOUP

Refreshing, tangy, and smooth — a good choice to serve as an appetizer or a dessert, as well as a soup course. This recipe also provides a fine way to use strawberries that are slightly past their prime. Garnish with sliced strawberries as the inn serves it or with whipped cream or yogurt and a sprig of mint.

1 quart strawberries, washed and hulled	1 cup sugar
1 cup white wine	4 tablespoons lemon juice
2 teaspoons grated lemon peel	Strawberry slices for garnish

Place all the ingredients in a blender or food processor and blend until smooth. Cover and chill for several hours or overnight. Serve in chilled bowls, garnished with strawberry slices. *Serves 6.*

THREE VILLAGE INN
Stony Brook, New York

COLD PLUM SOUP

Another lovely soup, this one a pastel purple. It makes a fine soup course for a summer meal or an unusual dessert to serve with crisp butter cookies.

1 can (29 ounces) purple plums	1 tablespoon cornstarch
1 cup water	2 tablespoons lemon juice
⅔ cup sugar	1 teaspoon grated lemon peel
1 cinnamon stick	1 cup sour cream
¼ teaspoon white pepper	3 tablespoons brandy
Pinch of salt	Sour cream and ground cinnamon for garnish
½ cup heavy cream	
½ cup dry red wine	

Drain the plums, reserving the syrup, then pit and chop them. In a medium saucepan combine the plums, syrup, water, sugar, cinnamon stick, white pepper, and salt. Bring to a boil over medium-high heat. Reduce the heat to medium and cook the mixture, stirring occasionally, 5 minutes. Stir in the heavy cream. Mix the red wine with the cornstarch and add, stirring constantly, until the mixture thickens. Stir in the lemon juice and grated lemon peel and remove from the pan.

In a small bowl whisk the 1 cup sour cream and brandy into ½ cup of the soup. Stir this mixture into the rest of the soup and stir the soup until smooth. Let the soup cool. Chill, covered, for at least 4 hours. Ladle the soup into cups or bowls and garnish each serving with a dollop of sour cream and a sprinkling of cinnamon. *Serves 6-8.*

HOT SOUPS

THE HULBERT HOUSE
Boonville, New York

CREAM OF CAULIFLOWER SOUP

An important flavoring in this soup is the chicken base, which restaurant kitchens tend to keep on hand. You can obtain it from any institutional food distributor open to the public. It's a great help in fortifying stocks, gravy, and dishes needing a good chicken flavor.

2 cups coarsely chopped
cauliflower florets
3 tablespoons butter or
margarine

3 tablespoons flour
4 cups milk
Pepper to taste
1 tablespoon chicken base

Cook the cauliflower in boiling salted water or steam it until tender. Melt the butter in a saucepan, stir in the flour, and cook over low heat for several minutes, stirring constantly. Slowly stir in the milk and bring just to a boil. Reduce the heat, add the cauliflower, and season with pepper. Stir in the chicken base. If the soup seems too thick, thin with additional milk to reach the desired consistency. *Serves 6-8.*

OLD DROVERS INN
Dover Plains, New York

CHEESE SOUP

This recipe came to the inn with its first chef in 1937 and has been a favorite on the menu ever since. It makes a rich soup to serve as a first course before a sauceless entrée or as a lunch dish with a hearty bread and a green salad. In very warm weather, serve it cold.

4 tablespoons butter
½ cup peeled, diced
  carrots
½ cup diced green pepper
½ cup minced onion
½ cup diced celery
⅓ cup flour

4 cups chicken stock
12 ounces white or yellow
  cheddar cheese, grated
3 to 3½ cups milk
Salt and pepper to taste
Chopped fresh chives or
  parsley for garnish

Melt the butter in the top of a double boiler. (Or use a heavy saucepan and cook over very low heat.) Add the vegetables and sauté until tender but not browned. Blend in the flour and cook, stirring constantly with a whisk, for several minutes. Add the stock and continue cooking, stirring constantly, until the mixture thickens. Strain. Stir in the cheese and cook, stirring constantly, until the cheese melts. Add enough milk to thin the mixture to the consistency of cream. Season with salt and pepper and garnish with chopped chives or parsley. Serve hot or cold.   *Serves 6-8.*

THE HORNED DORSET
Leonardsville, New York

BORSCHT

The texture of the shredded vegetables and the lovely color make this a special soup to serve on a cold day.

8 medium beets	1 pound ground beef
2 medium turnips	1 tablespoon dried thyme
3 medium carrots	1 tablespoon dried basil
1 gallon water	Salt and pepper to taste
1 can (28 ounces) peeled tomatoes, chopped	Sour cream and chopped fresh parsley
2 onions, finely chopped	
⅛ head red cabbage, shredded	

Put the beets, turnips, and carrots through a shoe-string grater. In a large soup pot bring the water to a simmer and add the grated vegetables. Add the tomatoes, onion, cabbage, ground beef, thyme, and basil to the water and simmer 30-45 minutes or until the vegetables are tender. Season with salt and pepper. Serve hot, with a dollop of sour cream and a sprinkling of fresh chopped parsley.   *Serves 12-14.*

THE BIRD & BOTTLE INN
Garrison, New York

BLACK BEAN SOUP

A hearty and satisfying soup, fine for lunch or supper on a cold winter day. Serve with homemade rye, whole-wheat, or corn bread. As a variation, add pieces of cooked ham to the soup. For extra flavor, use chicken stock instead of cold water.

1 package (12 ounces) dried turtle beans
2 ½ quarts (10 cups) cold water
1 cup chopped celery
2 cups chopped onion
¼ cup butter
4 teaspoons all-purpose flour
¼ cup chopped fresh parsley
Rind and bone from smoked ham

2 medium leeks, thinly sliced
2 bay leaves
1 ½ teaspoons salt
¼ teaspoon pepper
½ cup dry Madeira or sherry
Lemon slices and chopped hard-boiled egg for garnish

Wash and pick through the beans. Cover with boiling water and soak overnight. Drain and put in a large soup pot. Cover with cold water and bring to a boil. Reduce heat and simmer 1½ hours. In a frying pan slowly cook the celery and onion in the butter. Blend in the flour and cook over very low heat for several minutes. Add the parsley, and 2 cups of the beans and cooking liquid. Stir and add the mixture to the soup pot. Add the ham rind and bone, leeks, bay leaves, salt, and pepper. Cover and simmer 2½ hours or until the beans are completely cooked. Discard the rind, bone, and bay leaves. Drain the beans, reserving the broth, and put through a food mill or sieve. Return the broth and beans to the pot, stir in the Madeira or sherry, and heat thoroughly. Serve with a lemon slice and a sprinkling of hard-boiled egg.

Serves 8-10.

THE HULBERT HOUSE
Boonville, New York

MUSHROOM STEW

Reminiscent of sloppy joes, an easy dish for a casual supper. Serve with a tossed green salad.

2 pounds lean ground pork	2 cans (10¾ ounces each) tomato soup
2 to 3 green peppers, cored and chopped	1 can (10¾ ounces) water
¾ pound mushrooms, chopped	¼ cup ketchup (approximately)
2 onions, diced	Tabasco to taste
1 can (10 ounces) tomato sauce	

In a heavy skillet brown the pork until tender. Add the green peppers, mushrooms, and onions and simmer 10 minutes. Stir in the tomato sauce, tomato soup, and water and heat thoroughly. Add ketchup to the desired thickness and season with Tabasco. Serve in bowls or over rice. *Serves 8-10.*

THE POINT
Saranac Lake, New York

CHILIBEAN SOUP WITH CONDIMENTS

Spicy and tangy, a fine substitute for standard chili dishes. This is a hot dish, so reduce the spices to taste. It makes a complete meal served with rolls or bread and a salad.

2 tablespoons olive oil	1 to 2 teaspoons freshly
2 medium onions, diced	ground cayenne pepper
2 large red peppers, diced	4 teaspoons salt
2 large green peppers,	2 tablespoons brown
diced	sugar
4 teaspoons minced garlic	3 to 4 teaspoons
1 pound cooked steak, cut	Worcestershire sauce
into small cubes	1 strip lemon peel, 1 to 3
1 cup peeled, drained,	inches long
and diced tomatoes	1 teaspoon lemon zest
3 cups cooked red kidney	1 teaspoon crushed red
beans	pepper flakes
4 cups strong beef stock	Grated cheddar cheese
3 to 5 tablespoons chili	Sour cream
powder	Chopped green onions

Heat the oil in a large, deep, heavy pot. Sauté the onion and red and green peppers about 5 minutes. Stir in the garlic and sauté 5 minutes. Add the meat, tomatoes, beans, stock, chili powder, cayenne pepper, salt, brown sugar, Worcestershire sauce, and lemon peel. Stir occasionally and bring to a boil. Skim any foam from the surface and simmer over low heat 1 hour, stirring occasionally. Add the lemon zest and red pepper flakes. Adjust the seasoning to taste. (If the soup seems thin, add 1 tablespoon butter and 1 tablespoon flour mixed together.) Serve in soup crocks, with a tray of grated cheddar cheese, sour cream, and chopped green onions. *Serves 6.*

THE 1770 HOUSE
East Hampton, New York

RUSSIAN CABBAGE SOUP

This hearty, sweet-and-sour soup could make an entire meal if served with a wholesome bread. For a special garnish, top each bowl with a dollop of sour cream and finely chopped dill.

5 tablespoons vegetable oil	1 can (28 ounces)
2 large leeks (white part	tomatoes in purée
only), diced	4 cups chicken stock
2 carrots, peeled and	4 cups water
diced	½ cup brown sugar
2-pound brisket of beef	⅓ cup vinegar
12 cups shredded	2 tablespoons salt
cabbage, loosely packed	

Heat the oil in a large soup pot. Sauté the leeks and carrots until tender. Sear the meat over high heat and add to the pot along with the remaining ingredients. Cook, covered, over medium heat until the meat is tender, 2½-3 hours. When the meat is tender, remove it from the pot, refrigerate, and slice it thinly when cold. Reheat the soup and serve it with slices of meat or use the meat for another purpose. *Serves 12-14.*

GENESEE FALLS INN
Portageville, New York

CHICKEN NOODLE SOUP

Home-cooked noodles enhance this old favorite.

1 whole chicken	Chopped fresh parsley for
1 medium onion	garnish
1 medium carrot	Salt and pepper to taste
1 stalk celery	
Home-Cooked Noodles	
(recipe follows)	

Combine the chicken and vegetables in a soup pot, cover with water, and bring to a boil. Simmer, covered, until very tender, about 2 hours. Strain the liquid and reserve. Remove the chicken meat from the bones, chop, and reserve. (Stock might be concentrated; taste it and if desired, add some water and chicken base for flavor.) Prepare the noodles. Reheat the strained stock to simmering and drop in the noodles. Cook for several minutes until barely tender. Add the chopped chicken and chopped parsley and stir until heated through. Season with salt and pepper to taste.   *Serves 10-12.*

HOME-COOKED NOODLES

1½ cups flour	3 eggs, beaten
1 teaspoon salt	

Combine the flour and salt. Make a hollow in the flour and add the eggs. Mix well and knead about 40 times. Let rest 10 minutes. Divide the dough into small sections and roll each section out very thin. Cut into noodles of desired width.

KITTLE HOUSE
Mount Kisco, New York

CRAB CHOWDER

Brandy and sherry give this creamy, full-flavored chowder a wonderful richness. If using bottled clam juice, use half water and half juice.

8 cups clam stock	½ cup diced celery
1 cup dry sherry	3 tablespoons chopped
½ cup brandy	fresh thyme
¼ cup shallots	1 cup flour
1 tablespoon chopped	3 cups heavy cream
garlic	2 pounds crabmeat
8 stems fresh parsley	Coarse salt
4 bay leaves	Freshly ground white
4 medium potatoes, diced	pepper to taste
6 to 8 slices bacon, diced	Tabasco
2 cups diced red onions	

In a soup kettle or large Dutch oven combine the stock, sherry, brandy, shallots, garlic, parsley, and bay leaves. Bring to a boil, reduce heat, and simmer 20 minutes. Strain and reserve the stock. Cook the potatoes in a separate saucepan in boiling water and set aside. In the soup pot fry the diced bacon until crisp and remove from the pan. Add the onions and celery to the fat in the pan and sauté until tender. Add the thyme and flour and cook over low heat, stirring constantly, for several minutes. Slowly add the strained stock, whisking constantly, until the mixture is smooth. Stir in the cream and crabmeat and cook for several minutes until the chowder is hot. Season with coarse salt, white pepper, and Tabasco to taste.   *Serves 8-12*

DEPUY CANAL HOUSE
High Falls, New York

SCALLOP SOUP

This delectable soup is a feast for the eyes as well as the palate. It is a variation of a fish soup recipe given to chef John Novi by Craig Claiborne, food editor of The New York Times. Serve with a good French bread. Precede with a salad for a luncheon or reduce portions slightly and present as the soup course at a formal dinner. If desired, the soup can be made with snails rather than scallops.

2 tablespoons butter
1 teaspoon finely chopped garlic
¾ cup finely chopped onion
2 leeks (white part only), finely chopped
½ cup chopped heart of celery
1 cup diced carrots
1 medium sweet red pepper, diced
1 small green pepper, diced
1 hot pepper, diced (optional)

1 teaspoon powdered saffron
Fish sauce or salt to taste
Freshly ground pepper to taste
1 sprig fresh thyme
1 cup dry white wine
3 cups chicken stock
¾ cup cubed potatoes
1½ pounds sea scallops
2 cups heavy cream
8 bread croutons
¼ cup finely chopped fresh parsley

In a Dutch oven or soup pot heat the butter, add the garlic and onion, and cook until wilted. Add the leeks, celery, carrots, diced peppers, saffron, fish sauce or salt, ground pepper, and thyme. Cook approximately 3 minutes. Add the wine and chicken stock. Cover and cook approximately 5 minutes. Add the potatoes, cover, and cook approximately 10 minutes. Add the scallops and heavy cream. Bring just to the boiling point, reduce heat, and simmer 8 minutes. Ladle the soup into 8 bowls and top each with a crouton and chopped parsley. *Serves 8.*

ASA RANSOM HOUSE
Clarence, New York

PUMPKIN SOUP

As a special treat for your guests, serve this creamy, rich soup in a cleaned pumpkin shell that has been baked 10-15 minutes to heat it through.

1 cup diced onion	1 teaspoon crushed dried
1 cup diced celery	rosemary
1 cup (2 sticks) butter	Salt and pepper to taste
1 cup flour	2 tart apples, cored and
4 cups apple juice	diced
2 cups chicken stock	1 cup heavy cream
2 cups mashed, fresh	
pumpkin	

In a large kettle sauté the onion and celery in the butter until tender. Add the flour and cook, stirring constantly, 2-3 minutes. Heat the apple juice and chicken stock and slowly stir into the vegetables. Add the mashed pumpkin and simmer 10-15 minutes. Add the crushed rosemary and salt and pepper to taste. Add the diced apples and heavy cream and heat 5 minutes more.

Serves 10-12.

DEPUY CANAL HOUSE
High Falls, New York

SUNRISE SOUP
WITH CLOUDS OF GARLIC

Fish sauce, an ingredient found in specialty stores and Chinese groceries, varies in its saltiness from one manufacturer to another. Add it very slowly to the soup and taste as you go. You might not need as much as chef John Novi suggests for this most unusual soup.

Juice of 1 lemon
4 cups chicken broth
1 cup diced mushroom
    stems
2 scallions (white part
    only), finely chopped
2 tablespoons fish sauce
    (or less to taste)

6 tablespoons oil
2 large cloves garlic,
    minced
4 egg whites
2 dashes of Tabasco
6 egg yolks, at room
    temperature
Additional Tabasco

In a soup pot combine the lemon juice, chicken broth, mushroom stems, scallions, and fish sauce (to taste). Simmer. Heat the oil in a small pan, add the garlic, and sauté gently; do not brown. When the garlic is soft, remove from the heat and strain through a sieve, pressing the garlic until as much of its juice as possible is squeezed back into the oil in the pan. Reserve the oil. (This step can be done ahead of time, and the garlic oil can be refrigerated until you're ready to use it.) Beat the egg whites until soft peaks are formed. Add the 2 dashes of Tabasco and garlic oil to taste. Continue to beat the whites until the oil is fully blended. Spoon dollops of the egg white mixture into the simmering stock and poach on both sides until cooked. With a slotted spoon place one egg white cloud in each of 6 heated soup bowls (you might have a few extra clouds). Carefully ladle in the soup so the cloud floats to the top. Place an uncooked egg yolk in the center of each cloud. Serve with additional Tabasco. *Serves 6.*

THE 1770 HOUSE
East Hampton, New York

COUNTRY CARROT-PUMPKIN SOUP

A versatile soup with many variations: Use onions in place of leeks, thin with cream for a lighter consistency, add dry sherry to taste, or garnish with chopped chives.

½ cup (1 stick) unsalted butter
3 medium leeks (white part only), chopped
2 stalks celery, finely diced
4 large carrots, peeled and finely diced

1 cup fresh or canned puréed pumpkin
4 cups chicken stock
Salt and pepper to taste
Unsweetened whipped cream

Melt the butter in a large skillet or saucepan. Sauté the leeks, celery, and carrots in the butter until soft. Add the pumpkin, stock, and salt and pepper to taste. Stir until smooth. Simmer 30 minutes or until the vegetables are tender. Purée in a blender or food processor and adjust the seasonings. Garnish with a dollop of whipped cream. *Serves 8.*

LANZA'S COUNTRY INN
Livingston Manor, New York

PRIME RIB SOUP

A marvelous way to get every last bit of goodness from a prime rib roast.

Bones, fat, meat scraps, and leftover meat from 1 cooked prime rib (see cooking directions below)	3 to 4 cups chopped, cooked tomatoes and juice
2 cups chopped celery	1 bay leaf
2 cups chopped carrots	1 teaspoon thyme
2 cups chopped onion	1 tablespoon dried parsley
	Salt and pepper to taste

In a large soup pot combine all the prime rib leftovers and cover with water. Bring to a boil, reduce heat, and simmer 2 hours. Strain. Set the meat aside. Chill the stock. Remove all the good meat from the bones. Skim the fat from the chilled stock and discard. Return the stock to the pot. Add the celery, carrot, and onion and simmer until the vegetables are tender. Add the meat, tomatoes, herbs, and seasonings and simmer 1 hour longer. Remove the bay leaf and serve. *Serves 8-10.*

To Cook a Prime Rib Roast: Place the roast in a roasting pan, bone side down. Preheat the oven to 500°F. and sear the roast 15 minutes; reduce heat to 350°F. Roast 15 minutes per pound for rare, 20 minutes per pound for medium, and 25 minutes per pound for well done.

SALADS &
SALAD
DRESSINGS

Lanza's Country Inn, Livingston Manor, New York

ROUNDUP RANCH
Downsville, New York

SEAFOAM GELATIN SALAD

An old standby, this easy-to-make salad always disappears from a buffet table. Use other flavors of Jello for different color and taste. The following recipe is best served with sliced pineapple and a spiced apple ring as a garnish.

1 package lemon Jello	2 cups (16 ounces) cottage
1 package lime Jello	cheese
2 cups boiling water	1 cup evaporated milk
1 can (16 ounces) crushed	½ cup mayonnaise
pineapple	1 cup chopped walnuts

In a large bowl combine the Jello and boiling water. Set aside until cool but not firm. (If you're in a hurry, chill in the refrigerator for 10 minutes.) Add the pineapple, cottage cheese, evaporated milk, mayonnaise, and chopped walnuts to the cooled Jello. Pour the mixture into one large or several small molds. Chill overnight.   *Serves 12-14.*

COLGATE INN
Hamilton, New York

OATMEAL SALAD

Tasting a thousand times better than it sounds, this color-ful dish is a fine choice for a warm-weather brunch. It's a popular item on the inn's Sunday buffet menu. Use any fresh fruit in season or substitute canned fruit. The following recipe will serve at least 6 people, depending on how much fruit is added.

2 cups quick-cooking oatmeal	Sliced bananas
2 cups half-and-half	Grapes
½ cup honey	Orange segments
¼ cup raisins	Diced apple
	Walnut pieces for garnish

In a large bowl combine the oatmeal, half-and-half, honey, and raisins. Refrigerate overnight or at least 12 hours. Add the fruit in desired amounts and mix well. Serve garnished with walnuts.   *Serves at least 6.*

HUFF HOUSE
Roscoe, New York

TUNA MOLD

A tasty, firm salad that comes out of the mold a lovely pink color. Innkeeper Joanne Forness says her guests often think this is salmon mousse. Dip the mold in warm water for a few seconds to make unmolding easier.

2 envelopes unflavored
  gelatin
¼ cup cold water
1 can (10¾ ounces)
  tomato soup
1 package (8 ounces)
  cream cheese
1 cup mayonnaise
2 cans (7 ounces each)
  water-packed tuna,
  drained and flaked

Pinch of sugar
Pepper to taste
1 tablespoon lemon juice
1 medium onion, finely
  chopped
½ cup finely chopped
  celery

In a small bowl combine the gelatin and cold water, stir, and set aside. In a medium saucepan combine the tomato soup, cream cheese, and mayonnaise. Cook, stirring occasionally, over low heat until the cream cheese melts. Add the gelatin and water mixture. Mix well. Stir in the remaining ingredients and pour the mixture into a well-greased 5½-cup mold. Let set in the refrigerator. Unmold and serve on a bed of lettuce. *Serves 8.*

THE ATHENAEUM
Chautauqua, New York

THREE-BEAN SALAD

Easy to make, this versatile dish goes with just about anything. If you don't care for kidney beans substitute a can of corn with diced red peppers for color. This recipe also makes a nice marinade for fresh vegetables such as cucumbers, peppers, tomatoes, celery, or red onions.

½ cup sugar
½ cup oil
½ cup wine vinegar
Salt and freshly ground
  pepper to taste
½ cup chopped onions
½ cup chopped green
  peppers

1 can (16 ounces) cut
  green beans, drained
1 can (16 ounces) cut
  yellow beans, drained
1 can (16 ounces) red
  kidney beans, drained
3 cloves garlic

In a large container combine the sugar, oil, vinegar, and salt and pepper to taste. Stir until well blended. Add the remaining ingredients except the garlic and toss until evenly coated. Spear the garlic cloves with toothpicks and place in the salad. Chill, covered, at least 8 hours. Remove the garlic and serve. *Serves 6-8.*

ROUNDUP RANCH
Downsville, New York

CREAMY COLESLAW

Red cabbage makes this a lovely, colorful dish. Prepare the recipe in its entirety with a food processor. If cutting by hand, reduce the quantities to a more manageable amount. Serve with warm sesame bread sticks.

1 head red cabbage	3 cups mayonnaise
1 head green cabbage	3 tablespoons cider
6 carrots	vinegar
2 small green peppers,	2 tablespoons sugar
seeded	Salt and pepper to taste

Grate all the vegetables into a large bowl. In a small bowl combine the mayonnaise, vinegar, sugar, and salt and pepper to taste. Mix until smooth and frothy. Pour the dressing over the vegetables and mix well. Chill before serving. *Makes 10 cups.*

COLGATE INN
Hamilton, New York

SUMMER FRUIT SALAD
WITH HONEY-CINNAMON DRESSING

A fragrant and refreshing combination of flavors. Use whatever fruits are in season and consider packing this for a picnic or serving with fried chicken. By adding thinly sliced prosciutto and walnuts, the inn makes this salad a main luncheon entrée. It also can be served on a bed of lettuce or in a pineapple boat.

1 cup cubed cantaloupe
1 cup cubed honeydew
1 cup cubed pineapple
½ cup red or black grapes

½ cup peeled, sliced kiwi
½ cup mayonnaise
2 tablespoons honey
½ teaspoon cinnamon

Drain the fruit well and place in a large bowl. Set aside. In a small bowl combine the mayonnaise, honey, and cinnamon and blend until smooth. Pour the dressing over the fruit and toss well. Refrigerate until ready to serve. *Serves 4-6.*

LANZA'S COUNTRY INN
Livingston Manor, New York

WALNUT CHICKEN SALAD

The crunchy texture makes this a very special chicken salad, ideal for a hot-weather supper or lunch. The inn roasts the chicken with salt, pepper, and paprika and then chills the meat well before making the salad. You can also poach the chicken in simmering water or stock, let it cool, and then remove the meat from the bones.

2 to 3 cups cooked, cubed chicken	½ cup walnuts
½ cup chopped celery	Mayonnaise
2 tablespoons chopped onion	White seedless grapes for garnish

In a large bowl combine the chicken, celery, onion, and walnuts. Toss with just enough mayonnaise to hold the salad together. Garnish with grapes.   *Serves 6-8.*

HUFF HOUSE
Roscoe, New York

DELICIOUS TURKEY SALAD

A unique blend of wild rice, fresh vegetables, and succulent smoked turkey. Serve as a luncheon entrée or as an addition to a buffet table.

1 package (6 ounces)
  Uncle Ben's Original
  Long Grain and Wild
  Rice, uncooked
2 cups chopped, smoked
  turkey
¼ pound mushrooms,
  sliced
1 cup firmly packed
  spinach leaves, cut into
  thin strips

2 green onions with tops,
  sliced
⅓ cup dry white wine
¼ cup vegetable oil
2 teaspoons sugar
¼ teaspoon pepper
10 cherry tomatoes,
  halved

Cook the rice according to the directions on the package. Transfer to a large bowl and chill. Add the turkey, mushrooms, spinach, and green onions and mix well. In a small bowl combine the wine, oil, sugar, and pepper and blend well. Pour over the rice mixture and toss well. Chill. Just before serving add the tomatoes or arrange the tomatoes in a ring around the top.   *Serves 6.*

TAVERN ON THE GREEN
New York, New York

LOBSTER SALAD

A spectacular main dish, featuring, in addition to lobster, a colorful assortment of greens, vegetables, and fruit, with a tangy dressing. Serve with a good French bread.

1 head Bibb lettuce
1 head raddichio
2 heads Belgian endive
½ head frisee
½ bunch watercress
20 leaves mache
25 leaves arugula
Lobster Salad Dressing
 (recipe follows)
5 whole lobsters (1 pound each), boiled and cleaned (use tails and claws; slice the tail meat and leave the claws whole)
5 ounces fresh French green beans, blanched
15 shiitake mushroom caps
1 tablespoon very thinly sliced ginger root
1 scallion, thinly sliced
1 to 2 tablespoons oil or butter
3 cooked artichoke bottoms, cut into wedges
2 tomatoes, skinned, seeded, and julienned
15 orange segments
1 avocado, cut in half and thinly sliced
1 bunch chives, finely chopped

Place the mixture of greens in a large bowl. Pour on enough Lobster Salad Dressing to coat the leaves slightly. Arrange the greens on individual serving plates. Place the sliced meat from the lobster tails in a bowl with the green beans. Coat with the dressing and arrange on the greens. Sauté the mushrooms, ginger, and scallion in oil and cool slightly. Place the sautéed vegetables, artichoke bottoms, tomatoes, oranges, and avocado on the salad. Place the lobster claws on top and sprinkle with chives. Serve additional dressing on the side. *Serves 5.*

LOBSTER SALAD DRESSING

1 egg yolk
6 tablespoons Dijon
 mustard
1½ cups olive oil
¼ cup balsamic vinegar
¼ cup cider vinegar

1 teaspoon finely chopped
 garlic
1 teaspoon finely chopped
 shallot
Salt and pepper to taste

In a small bowl combine the egg yolk and mustard. Slowly add the oil, beating constantly. Add the balsamic and cider vinegar and continue beating. Add the garlic, shallot, and salt and pepper to taste.

GIDEON PUTNAM
Saratoga Springs, New York

SARATOGA AVOCADO DRESSING

Fresh mayonnaise, easily made in a blender, produces a dressing far superior to mayonnaise from a jar. If you can't make your own, double the amount of mustard in this recipe.

1 cup fresh mayonnaise
1 cup sour cream
2 teaspoons Dijon
 mustard
2 tablespoons red wine
 vinegar
2 tablespoons finely
 grated Parmesan cheese
Dash of Tabasco

1 teaspoon Worcestershire
 sauce
Juice of ½ lemon
½ teaspoon salt
¼ teaspoon white pepper
¼ teaspoon garlic powder
2 ripe avocados, peeled
 and puréed

In a mixing bowl combine all the ingredients except the avocados. Beat 3 minutes at medium speed or until mixture is smooth. Add the puréed avocados and beat 2 minutes more. Refrigerate if not used immediately.

Makes 2 cups.

BEEKMAN ARMS
Rhinebeck, New York

DIJON VINAIGRETTE

Great for salad and a fine marinade for fresh vegetables.

½ cup champagne vinegar
1 cup peanut oil
1 tablespoon whole-grain
  mustard
2 tablespoons Dijon
  mustard
1½ teaspoons minced
  shallot
1½ teaspoons chopped
  fresh lemon thyme

1½ teaspoons chopped
  fresh pineapple sage
¾ teaspoon coarsely
  ground pepper
1½ teaspoons poppy seeds
2 teaspoons honey
1 egg yolk, beaten

Combine all the ingredients except the egg yolk and mix well. Slowly blend in the beaten yolk, stirring constantly, until the dressing thickens.   *Makes 1¼ cups.*

BEEKMAN ARMS
Rhinebeck, New York

MUSTARD-DILL DRESSING

An old standby developed by a former executive chef at the inn, this dressing often is requested by guests.

1 cup mayonnaise
(preferably Hellmann's)
¼ cup Gulden's spicy
brown mustard
3 tablespoons whole-grain
mustard
2 tablespoons cider
vinegar

2½ tablespoons chopped
shallots
⅛ teaspoon fresh garlic
2½ tablespoons chopped
dill
½ cup sour cream

In a medium bowl combine all the ingredients and blend until smooth. *Makes 1½ cups.*

THE MERRILL MAGEE HOUSE
Warrensburg, New York

POPPY SEED DRESSING

Serve with a fresh fruit salad in half a pineapple shell.

1 cup honey
1 teaspoon salt
6 tablespoons vinegar
3 tablespoons Dijon
mustard

2 cups oil
2 tablespoons poppy seeds

In a small bowl mix the honey, salt, vinegar, and mustard. Gradually add the salad oil, beating well, until blended. Add the poppy seeds and mix again. Chill before serving. *Makes 3½ cups.*

BUTTERNUT INN
Chaffee, New York

SWEET BASIL DRESSING

A peppery, slightly sweet, and creamy mixture the inn features as its house dressing.

1½ cups mayonnaise
¼ cup light corn syrup
¼ cup finely chopped
  onion
3 tablespoons lemon juice

1½ tablespoons chopped
  fresh basil or 1
  teaspoon dried
½ teaspoon salt
¼ teaspoon pepper

Combine all the ingredients and mix well.
Makes 2 cups.

PLEASANT VIEW LODGE
Freehold, New York

BLUE CHEESE DRESSING

Once you try this recipe, you might never buy bottled blue cheese dressing again. Serve on greens or as a dip for raw vegetables. As an option, mix in cooked, chopped bacon.

10 ounces blue cheese
2 cups mayonnaise
1¼ cups sour cream
⅜ teaspoon salt
⅛ teaspoon pepper
⅛ teaspoon monosodium glutamate (optional)

¼ cup white vinegar
⅜ teaspoon Worcestershire sauce
Dash of Tabasco

Combine all the ingredients and mix well.

Makes 4½ cups.

ENTRÉES

Greenville Arms, Greenville, New York

POULTRY AND GAME

SHIP LANTERN INN
Milton, New York

CHICKEN BREAST FLORENTINE

A feast for the eyes and for the palate, achieving impressive results without hours of preparation. This dish can be made ahead, reheated, and sliced just before serving.

4 boneless chicken breasts
1 can (2 ounces)
  pimientos, chopped
1 teaspoon minced garlic
2 pounds ground veal
Salt and pepper to taste
1 can (16 ounces) spinach
  or 1 pound fresh
  spinach, cooked,
  drained, and chopped

Flour for dredging
4 tablespoons oil
Cheese Sauce (recipe
  follows)

Preheat oven to 350°F. Pound the chicken breasts until very flat. Set aside. Add the chopped pimientos and garlic to the ground veal, mix well, and season with salt and pepper. Layer the well-drained spinach on top of the pounded chicken. Shape the veal into cylinders, place one cylinder in the center of each spinach layer, and gently roll up the pounded breast, forming a "jellyroll" with the spinach and veal in the center. (To facilitate rolling, place plastic wrap under the breasts when pounding. Then grasp one edge of the plastic wrap and slowly raise it until the pounded veal rolls off.) Tie each roll in several places with butcher's twine or all-cotton cooking twine, then dredge in flour. In a large frying pan brown the rolls evenly on all sides in oil. Bake 40 minutes. Cool. Slice and serve with Cheese Sauce. *Serves 8-10.*

CHEESE SAUCE

½ cup (1 stick) butter	1 teaspoon chicken base
8 tablespoons flour	or bouillon
3 cups milk	3 tablespoons sherry
3 tablespoons grated cheese	

Melt the butter in a heavy saucepan, sprinkle in the flour, and cook over low heat, stirring constantly, for several minutes. Bring the milk to a boil and slowly stir into the butter and flour mixture until smooth. Add the grated cheese, chicken base or bouillon, and sherry and heat thoroughly. Spoon the sauce onto serving plates and arrange the slices of chicken on top. *Makes 4 cups.*

GLEN IRIS INN
Castile, New York

BREAST OF CHICKEN MICHAEL

Tender, golden chicken breasts filled with a savory, very colorful stuffing. Delicious served with cooked baby carrots.

½ cup Uncle Ben's
  Converted Rice,
  uncooked
1 cup chicken stock
¼ cup milk
Crumbs made from 1-
  pound loaf firm, white
  bread (crusts removed)
1 egg
2 tablespoons butter
1 shallot, minced
4 to 5 medium
  mushrooms, finely
  chopped
1 small clove garlic,
  minced
⅛ teaspoon dried thyme
Salt and pepper to taste
½ bay leaf

⅛ teaspoon dried
  rosemary
1 ½ teaspoons Madeira
¼ pound fresh spinach,
  cooked, drained, and
  chopped
½ pimiento, diced
2 tablespoons pine nuts,
  roasted
4 whole chicken breasts,
  boned, skinned, and
  halved
Flour for dredging
2 eggs beaten with 1
  tablespoon water
½ cup clarified butter
Madeira Sauce (recipe
  follows)

Cook the rice in the chicken stock and reserve. Scald the milk. Stir in 1 cup of the bread crumbs. Add the egg and stir. Set aside. Heat the butter in a saucepan and sauté the shallot until translucent. Add the mushrooms, garlic, thyme, salt and pepper to taste, bay leaf, and rosemary. Cook over low heat for several minutes. Add the Madeira, spinach, cooked rice, pimiento, and pine nuts. Cook for several minutes and stir in the bread mixture. Adjust the seasonings and cool.

Flatten the chicken breasts with a mallet. Spoon ¼ cup of the stuffing mixture onto each breast and fold in half. Working carefully, coat the breasts with flour, dip in the beaten eggs, and roll in the remaining bread crumbs. Preheat oven to 400°F. Sauté the breasts in the clarified butter until they are slightly browned. Remove to an ovenproof dish and bake approximately 20 minutes. Serve with Madeira Sauce. *Serves 8.*

MADEIRA SAUCE

1 cup chicken stock	½ cup heavy cream
2 tablespoons butter	2 tablespoons Madeira
3 tablespoons flour	

In a small saucepan bring the stock to a boil. Melt the butter in a heavy saucepan, stir in the flour, and cook over low heat, stirring constantly, for several minutes. Slowly stir in the boiling stock and simmer 10 minutes. Heat the cream and stir into the sauce. Strain. Add the Madeira, stir, and serve immediately.

Excellent ✗

GREENVILLE ARMS
Greenville, New York

CHICKEN CORDON BLEU
WITH RICE AND MUSHROOM SAUCE

These neat, self-contained packages of chicken, cheese, and ham in a tasty sauce go especially well with cooked rice. Both the chicken and the sauce reheat well, so you can prepare this dish in advance. You also can substitute Canadian bacon for the ham and use any type of imported Swiss cheese in place of the Gruyère, although it won't taste exactly the way it does at the inn.

3 chicken breasts, skinned, boned, and split	4 tablespoons grated Parmesan cheese
6 thin slices boiled or baked ham	¼ cup butter, melted
6 thin slices Gruyère cheese	Special Rice and Mushroom Sauce (recipes follow)
1 cup soft bread crumbs	

Preheat oven to 350°F. Flatten the chicken, using a mallet or rolling pin. Place one slice of ham and one slice of Gruyère cheese on each piece of chicken. Roll up like a jellyroll, folding in at the sides to hold the ham and cheese. Combine the bread crumbs with the Parmesan cheese. Dip each roll in melted butter and then into the crumbs and cheese. Arrange the rolls in a shallow baking dish or roasting pan and bake 40 minutes. As the chicken bakes, cook the Special Rice and prepare the Mushroom Sauce. *Serves 6.*

SPECIAL RICE

3 tablespoons butter	2 ½ cups hot water
½ cup sliced green onions	¼ cup chopped fresh
1 ¼ cups white rice,	parsley
uncooked	½ cup shredded carrots
3 chicken bouillon cubes	

Melt the butter in a 2-quart saucepan with a tight-fitting lid. Add the green onions and sauté until wilted. Add the rice and cook until it is opaque (about 3 to 5 minutes). Dissolve the bouillon cubes in the hot water and add to the rice. Cook over high heat until the mixture comes to a boil. Reduce heat and simmer 15-20 minutes or until the liquid is absorbed. Stir in the parsley and carrots.

MUSHROOM SAUCE

2 tablespoons butter	2 tablespoons chopped
1 pound fresh	fresh or freeze-dried
mushrooms, sliced	chives
1 can (10¾ ounces)	1 cup sour cream
condensed cream of	¼ cup chopped fresh
chicken soup	parsley
¼ cup milk	

In a heavy saucepan melt the butter and sauté the mushrooms until tender. Add the soup, milk, and chives and cook over medium heat, stirring occasionally, until the mixture comes to a boil. Remove from heat. Stir several tablespoons of the hot mixture into the sour cream. Stir the sour cream mixture into the remaining sauce in the pan. Warm over low heat. Just before serving, stir in the parsley and spoon the sauce over the chicken and rice.

GENEVA ON THE LAKE
Geneva, New York

BREAST OF CHICKEN JACQUELINE

An absolutely delectable, first-rate idea for chicken, blending a mellow, rich sauce with the slightly tart taste of apples. To save a little time, toast the almonds in the oven.

6 boned chicken breasts (6 ounces each), skinned
½ cup (1 stick) butter
¼ cup sliced almonds
Flour for dredging
Salt and freshly ground pepper to taste

¾ cup chicken stock (preferably unsalted)
¾ cup ruby port
1½ cups heavy cream
3 Granny Smith apples, peeled, cored, and cut into sixths

Cut out the white tendons from the undersides of the chicken and discard. Flatten each chicken breast slightly. Over medium heat melt 2 tablespoons of the butter in a small, heavy skillet. Add the almonds and cook over medium heat, stirring constantly, for about 4 minutes or until golden brown. Set aside. Season the flour with salt and pepper and lightly dredge the chicken in it; shake off all the excess flour. Melt 4 tablespoons of the butter in a large, heavy skillet, add the chicken, and cook over medium-high heat about 4 minutes per side or until springy to the touch. Transfer to a hot platter and cover with a foil tent.

Add the chicken stock and port to the cooking juices in the skillet and bring to a boil. Continue boiling, scraping up and incorporating into the sauce any browned bits from the sides until the liquid is reduced by one-half. Add the cream and bring to a boil again. Cook, stirring occasionally, until the mixture reaches a saucelike consistency. Meanwhile, melt the remaining 2 tablespoons butter in a heavy skillet. Add the apples and cook over medium heat, stirring frequently, 5 minutes or until just tender.

Arrange one chicken breast and three apple slices on each plate. Taste the sauce and season with salt and pepper. Pour the sauce over the chicken, sprinkle with almonds, and serve. *Serves 6.*

PLEASANT VIEW LODGE
Freehold, New York

CHICKEN ALMONDINE

This dish could become a family favorite, as it can be made in large quantities and prepared ahead of time. Cut into small pieces, the chicken also can be served as a party hors d'oeuvre or finger food. The following recipe yields about 48 cocktail tidbits.

2 eggs	4 chicken breasts, boned
1 cup milk	and skinned
½ to 1 cup flour	¼ cup butter
2 cups bread crumbs	1 lemon
1 cup sliced almonds	

Combine the eggs, milk, and flour and whip to form a smooth batter. Combine the bread crumbs and almonds. Cut the chicken breasts in half and pound until ¼ inch thick. Dip the chicken in the batter, then lay flat in the bread crumb mixture and pat crumbs on both sides. Heat the butter in a heavy skillet and brown. Sauté the breaded chicken in the brown butter until golden brown on both sides. Squeeze the lemon juice over the chicken and serve hot or chill and serve cold.   *Serves 8.*

TROUTBECK
Amenia, New York

CHICKEN MARINADE

Here's a full-flavored marinade to make chicken special, whether you bake it or broil it. The inn suggests experimenting and often uses cranberry juice instead of water. The following recipe will make enough marinade for 4 chickens. To create a sauce, simply thicken the mixture with cornstarch and pour it over the cooked chicken.

1 can (12 ounces)
   pineapple juice
1½ cups (12 ounces)
   water (use same
   amount of water as
   juice)
¼ cup brown sugar
1½ teaspoons minced
   garlic

1½ teaspoons minced
   ginger root
¼ cup tamari or soy sauce
4 tablespoons English
   chutney
4 tablespoons crushed
   pineapple
¼ cup sherry

Combine all the ingredients except the sherry in a large pot and bring to a boil. Add the sherry and pour the mixture over the chicken. Marinate overnight in the refrigerator.   *Makes 2 cups.*

DEBRUCE COUNTRY INN
DeBruce, New York

WANGHMANGHKYLL CHICKEN

If you have a wok, use it to prepare this dish, which features tender strips of chicken in a pungent, golden sauce. Once all the chopping and slicing is completed, the recipe comes together quickly. Red peppers make a colorful and tasty addition.

4 cups chicken bouillon
2 cups rice
1 whole chicken breast, boned and skinned, cut into thin strips
5 tablespoons soy sauce
1 tablespoon sugar
5 to 10 cloves garlic, chopped
¼ teaspoon curry powder
2 tablespoons cornstarch
4 tablespoons oil

1 large onion, chopped
1 small zucchini, quartered lengthwise and cut into ¼-inch-thick pieces
2 stalks celery, cut into ¼-inch-thick slices
½ cup sliced mushrooms
1 tablespoon minced fresh ginger
1 can (8 ounces) pineapple chunks, with juice

In a large saucepan bring the bouillon to a boil. Stir in the rice, cover, and return to a boil. Reduce the heat and cook until the liquid is absorbed, about 20 minutes. Combine the chicken strips, 1 tablespoon of the soy sauce, 1-1½ teaspoons of the sugar, and the chopped garlic in a medium bowl. Set aside. Sprinkle the curry powder over the chicken and mix well. In a separate bowl mix the cornstarch with 2 tablespoons of the soy sauce and set aside.

Heat 2 tablespoons of the oil in a large skillet or wok over high heat. Sauté the chicken mixture and onion in the hot oil until browned. Remove from the skillet. Heat the remaining 2 tablespoons oil in the same skillet. Stir in the zucchini, celery, and mushrooms and cook until lightly browned. Add the ginger, the remaining 1-1½ teaspoons sugar, the remaining 1 tablespoon soy sauce, and the pineapple chunks and juice. Stir well. Add the cornstarch mixture and stir. Return the chicken and onions to the skillet. Stir until the sauce thickens. Serve with the rice.   *Serves 4-6.*

WINTER CLOVE INN
Round Top, New York

WINTER CLOVE BREAST OF CHICKEN

A light and delicate dish, with spinach providing a color-ful bed. Serve with additional sauce on the side. For more color, garnish each serving with sprigs of parsley.

2 tablespoons butter	¼ teaspoon garlic powder
2 teaspoons finely chopped onion	2 tablespoons dry sherry
½ cup chopped mushrooms	2 cups bread cubes or bread crumbs
½ cup finely chopped celery	1 egg, beaten
2 teaspoons chopped fresh parsley	6 boned chicken breasts (5 ounces each)
1 teaspoon salt	3 cups cooked, well drained, fresh spinach
½ teaspoon pepper	Mushroom Sauce (recipe follows)

Melt the butter in a large skillet and sauté the onion, mushrooms, and celery until tender. Stir in the parsley, salt, pepper, garlic powder, and sherry. Add the bread cubes or crumbs and the beaten egg and mix gently. Preheat oven to 350°F. Place the chicken breasts over portions of the stuffing. Roast the chicken 30 minutes or until tender. Serve on a nest of spinach, topped with Mushroom Sauce. *Serves 6.*

MUSHROOM SAUCE

1 tablespoon butter	½ cup white wine
½ cup chopped	(preferably Chablis)
mushrooms	1 tablespoon
1 tablespoon flour	Worcestershire sauce
3 cups chicken stock	1 cup sour cream
½ cup orange juice	

Melt the butter in a heavy skillet and sauté the mushrooms until barely tender. Sprinkle with the flour and cook over low heat, stirring gently, for several minutes. Slowly add the chicken stock, orange juice, white wine, and Worcestershire sauce. Stir until smooth and cook several minutes over medium heat. Stir in the sour cream and heat thoroughly.

THE CONCORD
Kiamesha Lake, New York

CHICKEN DIJONNAISE

Since The Concord is a kosher establishment, chef James Farina does not mix dairy products with meat and prepares the sauce for this recipe with mocha, a nondairy creamer. Here we present a variation of his recipe, using light cream and preparing the sauce separately. Chef Farina's instructions follow at the end of the recipe.

1½ chickens, cut into pieces, or 4 pounds chicken parts	2 tablespoons white wine
	3 tablespoons butter
	3 tablespoons flour
3 tablespoons Dijon mustard	1 tablespoon dry mustard
2 tablespoons dry vermouth	1 cup light cream or mocha

Place the chicken in a shallow pan or bowl and coat well with Dijon mustard. Marinate at room temperature 2 hours. Preheat oven to 350°F. Sprinkle the marinated chicken with vermouth and white wine and bake 1 hour or until done. Remove the chicken to a heated platter and keep warm. Pour 1 tablespoon of the pan juices into a saucepan (or make the sauce directly in the baking dish). Add the butter and stir over low heat until the butter melts. Slowly add the flour and dry mustard and cook over low heat for several minutes, stirring constantly, until the mixture thickens. Slowly add the light cream, stirring to form a smooth, thick gravy. Pour the gravy over the chicken and serve. *Serves 6-8.*

As Served at The Concord: After marinating the chicken 2 hours, remove the excess mustard and make a sauce using mocha, the roux, and dry mustard. Pour the sauce over the chicken and sprinkle with white wine and vermouth. Bake 45 minutes, basting frequently. Remove the chicken from the pan and strain the sauce to remove excess fat. Pour the sauce over the chicken and serve.

SNAPPER INN
Oakdale, New York

CHICKEN AUTUMN MEDLEY

Cranberries add a pleasing bit of color to this quick and easy dish, which the inn serves on a bed of rice.

2 whole chicken breasts, boned and skinned	½ cup fresh cranberries
Flour for dredging	2 tablespoons red currant jelly
Salt and pepper to taste	1 cup chicken stock
2 to 4 tablespoons clarified butter	½ cup chopped, cooked chestnuts
2 tablespoons dry white wine	

Cut the chicken into bite-size pieces. Season the flour with salt and pepper and dredge the chicken in it. In a large skillet heat the clarified butter and sauté the chicken, turning to brown all sides, about 2 minutes per side. Add the white wine and stir to deglaze the pan. Then add the cranberries, currant jelly, and chicken stock and season with salt and pepper. Bring to a boil, reduce the heat, and simmer 4-5 minutes. Add the chestnuts, cook 1 minute longer, and remove from heat.   *Serves 4.*

MOHONK MOUNTAIN HOUSE
New Paltz, New York

CHICKEN CACCIATORE

A hearty dish that's very simple to make and tastes good enough to serve your company. If you don't have a skillet large enough for all the pieces, brown the chicken in batches, place it in a 9x15-inch casserole dish, and bake at 350°F. for 45 minutes.

4 cups peeled, chopped tomatoes
2 broiler chickens, cut into pieces
Flour for dredging
2 teaspoons salt
½ cup fat
¼ cup chopped onion
1 clove garlic, finely chopped
¼ cup chopped carrot
3 sprigs parsley, chopped
1 bay leaf or basil leaf
Dash of pepper
¼ cup Marsala, sherry, or dry white wine

Push the tomatoes through a strainer (they will yield approximately 2 cups of pulp). Dredge the chicken in flour and sprinkle with 1 teaspoon of salt. In a very large skillet melt the fat and brown the chicken until golden on both sides. Place in a covered dish and keep warm. In the remaining fat brown the onion, garlic, carrot, parsley, and bay leaf or basil leaf. Add the tomato pulp to the browned vegetables along with the remaining 1 teaspoon of salt and a dash of pepper. Bring to a boil, add the chicken and wine, and simmer 30 minutes or until the chicken is tender. Remove the bay leaf and serve.

Serves 6-8.

THE ATHENAEUM
Chautauqua, New York

CHICKEN ALBA

An elegant dish to serve for a small dinner party.

Apricot preserves	2 to 3 cups Bisquick
6 whole chicken breasts, boned and flattened	Salt and pepper to taste
	Endive
12 broccoli spears, blanched	Apricot Glaze (recipe follows)

Preheat oven to 350°F. Spread the apricot preserves over the meat side of the breasts. Arrange two broccoli spears in the center of each. Roll up the chicken securely. Combine the Bisquick with the salt and pepper to taste. Dredge the rolled breasts in the mixture. Place in a shallow baking dish. Bake 45-60 minutes until golden brown. To serve, place on a bed of endive and top with Apricot Glaze.   *Serves 6.*

APRICOT GLAZE

3 cups apricot preserves   1 cup water

Press the preserves through a sieve. In a heavy saucepan combine the strained preserves and the water. Cook over medium heat for several minutes, stirring constantly, until smooth.

TRYON INN
Cherry Valley, New York

INNKEEPER'S CHICKEN

Artichoke hearts dress up this dish, which can easily be served as a family meal, along with rice and a salad.

Flour for dredging
Salt and pepper to taste
4 chicken breasts (8 ounces each), boned and skinned
6 tablespoons butter
¼ cup chopped green pepper
¼ cup chopped onion
¼ cup chopped celery
1 clove garlic, minced
½ cup sliced mushrooms
1 can (14½ ounces) stewed tomatoes
¼ cup white wine
1 jar (8 ounces) artichoke hearts, drained

Preheat oven to 350°F. Season the flour with salt and pepper. Dredge the chicken breasts in the flour. Melt 2 tablespoons of the butter in a heavy skillet and sauté the chicken until it is golden brown. Remove from the pan and place in an ovenproof baking dish. Melt the remaining 4 tablespoons butter in the skillet and sauté the pepper, onion, celery, and garlic for several minutes. Add the mushrooms and sauté until the vegetables are tender but not brown. Remove pan from the heat. Stir in the tomatoes, wine, and artichoke hearts. Pour the mixture over the chicken in the baking dish and bake 20-25 minutes or until the chicken is thoroughly cooked. *Serves 4.*

SNAPPER INN
Oakdale, New York

CHICKEN LOUISE

An easy recipe with enjoyable results. Serve any extra sauce over steamed vegetables, such as broccoli.

4 whole, boned chicken breasts, cut in halves and pounded thin
Flour for dredging
2 tablespoons clarified butter
4 shallots, peeled and diced

½ cup dry white wine
1½ cups heavy cream
1 can (15 ounces) medium straw mushrooms, drained
Salt and white pepper to taste
Chopped fresh parsley

Dredge the flattened chicken in flour and shake off any excess. In a large, heavy skillet heat the clarified butter and sauté the chicken for several minutes on each side until lightly browned. Remove the chicken from the pan. Add the shallots and sauté until soft. Deglaze the pan with the white wine. Add the cream, mushrooms, and salt and pepper to taste. Cook 15-20 minutes, stirring frequently, until the sauce is reduced by about one-quarter and easily coats the back of a spoon. Add the chicken and heat for another minute. Serve sprinkled with fresh parsley. *Serves 4.*

SNAPPER INN
Oakdale, New York

NEW ENGLAND CHICKEN WITH APPLE CIDER SAUCE

You can make this dish at any time of the year, but it deserves to be served in the fall.

4 whole, boned chicken
  breasts, pounded thin
Snapper Inn Stuffing
  (recipe follows)
Flour for dredging
1 egg beaten with ⅓ cup
  milk

Bread crumbs
2 to 4 tablespoons
  clarified butter
Apple Cider Sauce (recipe
  follows)

Preheat oven to 375°F. Lay the flattened breasts on a flat surface. Divide the stuffing among the 4 breasts and spoon it into the center of each. Wrap the chicken around the stuffing. Carefully dredge the stuffed breasts in flour, then dip them in the egg and milk mixture, and roll in bread crumbs. Flatten slightly. In a large, heavy skillet heat the clarified butter until hot. Sauté the chicken until browned on both sides. Remove from the pan and place in a shallow dish. Bake 15 minutes or until cooked through. Serve topped with Apple Cider Sauce.

Serves 4.

SNAPPER INN STUFFING

½ cup white seedless
   grapes
½ cup red seedless grapes
¼ cup raisins
1 Granny Smith apple,
   cored and diced

1 teaspoon cinnamon
¼ teaspoon salt
Pinch of nutmeg
½ cup bread crumbs

In a strainer over boiling water steam the grapes, raisins, and apple 3 minutes, covered. Remove and combine with the cinnamon, salt, and nutmeg. Stir in the bread crumbs and mix well. Set aside to cool.

APPLE CIDER SAUCE

1 cup apple cider
½ cup chicken stock
2 tablespoons currant jelly

1 tablespoon cornstarch
   (or more)
1 cup applesauce

In a medium saucepan combine the cider, chicken stock, and currant jelly. Bring the mixture to a boil. Thicken with cornstarch. (Add a bit more cider if necessary.) Remove from the heat and stir in the applesauce.

KITTLE HOUSE
Mount Kisco, New York

CHICKEN ARMAGNAC

A fine way to dress up chicken. Take your time slicing the leek by hand or with a food processor, as it is an important part of the dish's visual appeal.

1 chicken breast (8 to 10 ounces), skinned and boned
Flour for dredging
2 tablespoons clarified butter
1 shallot, diced
1 leek, julienned

½ medium tomato, diced
6 broccoli florets
2 tablespoons crabmeat
¼ cup Armagnac
¼ cup heavy cream
Salt and freshly ground pepper to taste

Trim and flatten the chicken. Dredge it in the flour. In a heavy skillet heat the clarified butter until hot and sauté the chicken for several minutes on each side. Drain off most of the butter. Add the shallot, leek, tomato, and broccoli and cook for several minutes until the vegetables are just tender. Add the crabmeat and Armagnac. Flame. Cook over medium-high heat until the liquid in the pan is reduced by one-half. Add the cream and cook several minutes until the sauce is thickened. Season with salt and freshly ground pepper. Serve immediately.

Serves 1.

ROUNDUP RANCH
Downsville, New York

PERFECT BUFFET TURKEY

This advice was given to us by June Kilpatrick. It's simple yet makes a big difference in serving turkey.

Bake a turkey stuffed with your favorite dressing according to your favorite recipe. Remove the stuffing. Put a tea towel over the turkey to keep it from drying out and refrigerate it until well chilled. Remove the towel and start carving. First, slice the skin from front to back through the breast bone. Carefully remove the skin from the breast on both sides, folding it over the drumstick and wing. Be careful to avoid ripping the skin and exposing the whole breast. Next, carefully cut out the breast meat in one piece.

Slice the breast meat, keeping slices in the same order that you remove them. Place the meat back on the side from which you cut it. Fold the skin back over the breast and secure it with toothpicks. Position cherry tomatoes on the toothpicks and garnish with parsley to camouflage the breastbone cut.

TROUTBECK
Amenia, New York

ROAST LONG ISLAND DUCKLING WITH BIGARADE SAUCE

This recipe will keep you in the kitchen for some time and will expose you to some very unusual ingredients for stock, but the results are well worth the effort. Undercook the ducks somewhat so they don't become stringy when reheated. If you have leftover sauce, freeze it and use that fine flavor for another dish.

3 ducklings (4 to 5 pounds each)
Pickling spice
3 bananas, peeled
3 oranges, peeled
3 limes, peeled
½ cantaloupe, seeded and peeled
¼ cup chopped fresh parsley

¼ cup onion skins
2 cups cider vinegar
2 cups sugar
2 cups currant jelly
½ cup flour
¼ cup Grand Marnier
2 tablespoons dry sherry
2 tablespoons sweet cream sherry

Preheat oven to 425°F. Remove the wings from the ducks at the first joint, trim any excess fat from both ends, and remove the neck giblets. Save all these parts. Sprinkle the ducks with pickling spice. Roast on wire

racks 1½ hours or until the leg bones move when lifted.
Cool. Drain the fat and reserve. In a large soup kettle
make a stock by combining the giblets, fat, and trimmings, along with the bananas, oranges, limes, cantaloupe, parsley, and onion skins. Simmer over low heat 2
hours. (You should have approximately ½ gallon.)

Bone the ducks, holding the carcass in one hand. Cut
the skin over the breast. Using the inside of your hand,
carefully separate the carcass from the meat. (You will
have to pinch or cut the joint by the wing bone.) Remem-
ber to keep the skin and meat intact. Add the carcass to
the stock. Simmer 20 minutes, strain, and cool. Remove
the fat. (This can be done a day ahead.) Reserve the
oranges, scrape off and discard the white pulp, and cut
into thin strips. Set aside.

In a heavy saucepan combine the vinegar with the
sugar and cook over low heat until the sugar dissolves.
Continue cooking until the mixture reaches the soft-ball
stage (a drop in a cup of cold water will form a soft ball).
Carefully add the currant jelly. Let cool slightly and slowly add to the strained stock.

In a second saucepan melt ¼ cup of duck fat. Add the
flour and cook over low heat, stirring constantly, until
the mixture is thick. Continue cooking until it is the
consistency of wet sand. Use to thicken the hot stock
until the sauce coats a spoon. Add the Grand Marnier,
dry sherry, cream sherry, and reserved orange strips.
Check seasonings. To serve, reheat the duck in a hot
oven (350°-400°F.) 6-8 minutes. Place servings on rice and
spoon sauce over the top.   *Serves 6.*

AUBERGE DES 4 SAISONS
Shandaken, New York

LAPIN AU VIN BLANC

Rabbit in white wine has been a regular item on the Auberge's menu for nearly 30 years. This recipe was passed on to the present innkeepers by Dadou Labeille and Chef Pierre Faur, who still prepares rabbit as he has for many years. The inn recommends serving the rabbit garnished with quartered mushrooms sautéed in butter and with pearl onions boiled in lightly salted water. The rabbit's liver also can be sautéed and sliced for garnish. Serve with a lightly buttered pasta, such as linguine, and a green vegetable.

1 rabbit (3 to 4 pounds)	1 teaspoon fresh rosemary
1 carrot, sliced	3 cloves garlic, crushed
1 stalk celery, sliced	1 bottle dry white wine
1 yellow onion, sliced	3 tablespoons clarified
2 teaspoons fresh thyme	butter or peanut oil
4 bay leaves	3 shallots, chopped
Several sprigs Italian	3 tablespoons flour
parsley	1½ cups chicken stock

Cut the rabbit into serving pieces. In a glass dish combine the carrot, celery, onion, half the herbs, the crushed garlic, and the wine. Add the rabbit and marinate overnight, turning once or twice in the marinade. Remove the rabbit from the marinade and pat dry. Strain the marinade and reserve. In a heavy skillet heat the clarified butter or oil until hot and sauté the rabbit pieces until well browned on all sides. Stir in the shallots. Add the flour and stir. Add the strained marinade, the remaining herbs, and the chicken stock. Simmer, covered, 45-60 minutes until the rabbit is tender. Remove the rabbit to a warm serving plate, strain the stock into a medium saucepan, and reduce it by one-half over medium-high heat. Pour over the rabbit pieces and serve.   *Serves 6-8.*

LE CHAMBORD
Hopewell Junction, New York

MAGRET DE CANARD

A most unusual sauce, using heavy cream and your favorite kind of loose tea.

1 duck breast	½ cup heavy cream
4 tablespoons olive oil	2 teaspoons loose tea (any
½ cup red wine	flavor)
2 tablespoons chopped	1 tablespoon glace of duck
shallots	stock
1 garlic clove, crushed	1 teaspoon Grand
½ bay leaf	Marnier
2 sprigs parsley	Salt and pepper to taste

Place the duck breast in a glass container. Combine the olive oil, red wine, carrot, shallots, garlic, bay leaf, and parsley. Pour over the breast and marinate 3 days. Wipe the breast dry and broil. Slice it very thin. In a heavy saucepan cook the cream until slightly reduced. Add the tea and continue cooking until reduced by one-third. Strain. Add the glace, Grand Marnier, and salt and pepper to taste. Reduce again. Spoon the sauce over the duck slices and serve immediately.   *Serves 1.*

FISH AND SEAFOOD

GIDEON PUTNAM
Saratoga Springs, New York

FROGS LEGS PROVENÇALE

Not your typical pantry fare, but this is a fine way to prepare a dish many consider a delicacy. The inn serves them with garlic bread.

8 pairs of frogs legs,
   separated at the hips
Flour seasoned to taste
   with salt and pepper
¼ cup butter
1 tomato, diced

2 cloves garlic, minced
1 teaspoon chopped fresh
   parsley
½ cup dry white wine
¼ cup water
Salt and pepper to taste

Dredge the frogs legs in flour. In a sauté pan large enough to hold all the legs in one layer melt the butter and sauté the legs over medium heat for 2 minutes on each side or until brown. Add the diced tomato, garlic, and parsley and cook 3-4 minutes longer, turning once. Add the wine and water, reduce the heat, and cook an additional 3 or 4 minutes. Season with salt and pepper.

Serves 2.

THE 1770 HOUSE
East Hampton, New York

COLD POACHED SALMON
WITH THREE RIBBON SAUCE

A very elegant and impressive dish, fine enough to celebrate a wedding. If poaching a whole salmon makes the recipe too expensive for your budget, substitute fillets of salmon or salmon steaks and adjust the poaching time according to the size of your fish. Leaving the head and tail on makes this a traditional dish; remove them if you must.

3 quarts court-bouillon   3 stalks celery with tops
(equal parts of chicken   2 tablespoons salt
stock and water,   1 whole salmon (8 to 9
seasoned if desired with   pounds), cleaned
vermouth)   Three Ribbon Sauce
Parsley to taste   (recipe follows)

Prepare the court-bouillon, then pour the liquid into a large pan or fish poacher. Add a few sprigs of parsley, the celery, and the salt. Bring the liquid to a boil and simmer 10 minutes. Wrap the salmon in cheesecloth and place it on a rack in the liquid. Cover (use foil to make a cover if your container does not have a tight-fitting lid) and poach either on top of the stove or in a 375°F. oven for 1 hour. Carefully remove the fish and cool. When cool, unwrap, carefully peel off the skin, and serve with Three Ribbon Sauce.   *Serves 20-30.*

(continued on next page)

(continued from preceding page)

THREE RIBBON SAUCE

Prepare the following three sauces, tasting as you add the herbs and seasonings, to come up with just the right spiciness for your palate. All of them can be prepared in advance; just refrigerate until mealtime. Serve the fish on a large, oval platter with the sauces spooned in rings around it. For contrast, put the Salsa Verde next to the fish, add a ring of Dill Sauce, then add the Remoulade Sauce as the outside ring. Also consider serving the fish in individual portions on small, round plates with the sauces spooned in concentric rings around each portion.

Salsa Verde (Green Sauce)

1 cup (2 sticks) butter, softened
2 hard-boiled eggs, chopped
2 tablespoons olive oil
2 cloves garlic, mashed
10 spinach leaves

6 sprigs parsley
2 shallots, chopped
3 tablespoons capers
½ teaspoon dry mustard
Lemon juice to taste
Salt and pepper to taste

Place the butter, eggs, oil, and garlic in a blender and blend until smooth. In a medium saucepan blanch the spinach, parsley, and shallots by covering them with water and bringing them to a boil for several minutes until the vegetables are wilted. Drain well and add to the butter mixture. Add the capers and dry mustard. Blend again and add the lemon juice and salt and pepper to taste. This sauce can be prepared ahead of time, refrigerated, and warmed just until it liquefies again.

Remoulade Sauce (Red Sauce)

1 ½ cups mayonnaise   ¼ cup horseradish
¾ cup chili sauce

Combine all the ingredients and stir until smooth.

Sour Cream Dill Sauce (White Sauce)

2 cups sour cream   1 tablespoon horseradish
1 cup mayonnaise   ½ cup chopped fresh dill
1 tablespoon Dijon
   mustard

Combine all the ingredients and stir until smooth.

TRYON INN
Cherry Valley, New York

SALMON IN LEMON-CREAM SAUCE

The delicate flavor of salmon is pleasantly enhanced by the mild, lemony sauce, and the colors of pink and yellow make this dish especially pleasing to the eye. Serve with a green vegetable and rice or pasta.

1 cup heavy cream	2 salmon steaks (8 ounces
1 tablespoon finely	each)
chopped onion	Lemon slices and fresh
Juice of 1 lemon	parsley for garnish
Salt and pepper to taste	

In a small bowl combine the cream, onion, lemon juice, and salt and pepper to taste. Refrigerate 30 minutes. Preheat oven to 375°F. Place the salmon steaks in a buttered baking dish and pour the sauce over them. Bake the salmon 20-25 minutes until it is flaky but not dry. Be careful not to overcook. If the sauce is too thin for your taste, pour it off into a small saucepan. Keep the salmon warm while you cook the sauce over medium heat until it reaches the desired consistency. Spoon it over the salmon and serve. Garnish with lemon slices and parsley. *Serves 2.*

THE POINT
Saranac Lake, New York

GRILLED SALMON STEAK
WITH MUSTARD HERB SAUCE

Salmon in a tangy sauce, just right for a small, elegant dinner party.

3 tablespoons oil
18 tablespoons sweet
  butter
4 salmon steaks (6 ounces
  each), boned
3 tablespoons chopped
  shallots
1 tablespoon chopped
  fresh tarragon
1 tablespoon chopped
  fresh dill

1 tablespoon chopped
  fresh chives
½ cup dry sherry
½ cup heavy cream
2 to 3 tablespoons Dijon
  mustard
Salt and pepper to taste
Fresh tarragon and dill
  sprigs for garnish

Preheat oven to 400°F. In a large skillet heat the oil and 2 tablespoons of the butter until hot. Sauté the salmon on both sides until brown. Remove to a baking dish and bake 15 minutes. Drain the oil from the skillet and sauté the shallots until golden brown. Add the tarragon, dill, and chives and deglaze the pan with the sherry. Add the cream and cook over medium heat until the liquid is reduced by one-half. Cut the remaining butter into cubes and whisk it into the sauce, a few pieces at a time. Whisk in the mustard. Do not let the sauce boil. Adjust the seasoning with salt and pepper. Spoon some sauce onto a serving plate to form a pool. Place the salmon steak in the pool and garnish with fresh tarragon and dill. *Serves 4.*

ASA RANSOM HOUSE
Clarence, New York

HADDOCK WITH HERB RICE

Savory rice and tender fish fillets in a tangy lemon sauce.
A good family dish to serve with a green vegetable or a salad.

½ cup diced celery	3¾ cups chicken stock
½ cup diced onion	2 teaspoons salt
½ cup diced carrot	½ teaspoon pepper
¼ cup oil	2 pounds thin haddock
1½ cups brown rice,	fillets, skinned
uncooked	¼ cup butter
1 bay leaf	¼ cup flour
1 teaspoon dried thyme	¼ cup lemon juice
½ teaspoon dried dill	

In a large, ovenproof skillet sauté the diced celery, onion, and carrot in oil until soft. Add the brown rice, bay leaf, thyme, and dill and stir to coat the rice with oil. Heat 3 cups of the chicken stock and add to the rice along with the salt and pepper. Preheat oven to 350°F. Bring the mixture to a boil and bake in the oven 30-45 minutes or until all the liquid is absorbed. Check the seasoning. Place the hot rice in a large baking dish and cover with the haddock fillets. Bake 10 minutes longer. As the fish bakes, melt the butter in a heavy saucepan over low heat. Sprinkle with flour and cook several minutes, stirring constantly. Slowly add the remaining ¾ cup stock and lemon juice, bring just to a boil, and cook several more minutes, stirring constantly, until the sauce is smooth. Spoon the sauce over the fish and rice.   *Serves 5-6.*

SNAPPER INN
Oakdale, New York

FLOUNDER AVOCADO

Avocado darkens as it cooks, so be sure to cover the fillets generously with bread crumbs to avoid an unpleasant color.

2 ripe avocados	6 large flounder fillets
1 shallot, peeled	Bread crumbs
Juice of ½ lemon	Paprika to taste
Salt and pepper to taste	Chopped fresh parsley
¼ cup butter, softened	

Preheat oven to 375°F. Cut the avocados in half lengthwise, remove the pits, and peel. In a food processor combine 1 avocado with the shallot, lemon juice, and salt and pepper to taste. Purée until smooth. Add the softened butter and mix well. Cut the remaining avocado halves into thirds, making 6 wedges. Roll 1 flounder fillet around each wedge and place the rolls in a deep baking dish. Place the dish in a pan of hot water. Top each fillet with a spoonful of avocado butter and cover with a layer of bread crumbs. Sprinkle with paprika. Bake 15-20 minutes. Remove from the oven. Sprinkle with parsley and serve immediately. *Serves 6.*

DEBRUCE COUNTRY INN
DeBruce, New York

DEBROSSES TROUT

The DeBrosses are an old New York family and local landowners for whom the hamlet of DeBruce is named. The inn prepares this recipe with a trout that has been gutted through the mouth, a process your fish monger might not know how to do. If you can't obtain a trout cleaned this way, you can sew up the side once it is stuffed. If sorrel leaves aren't available, use watercress and a splash of lemon juice.

1 whole dressed trout
DeBruce Stuffing (recipe
  follows)
5 whole lettuce leaves (use
  loose-leaf lettuce),
  blanched
2 tablespoons butter,
  melted

Court-Bouillon (recipe
  follows)
1 teaspoon cornstarch or
  arrowroot
1 tablespoon water
Lemon wedges for garnish

Preheat oven to 450°F. Fill the fish cavity with DeBruce Stuffing and sew up with a needle and thread if necessary. On the bottom of a fish poacher rack arrange the blanched lettuce leaves so they overlap and completely cover the bottom. Place the fish on top of the leaves. Pull the leaves up to cover the fish completely. Brush both sides of the fish with melted butter. Pour the Court-Bouillon into the bottom of the poacher, cover tightly, and bake 20-25 minutes. Transfer the fish to a warmed platter. If used, remove sewing thread. Strain the liquid from the poacher into a heavy saucepan. Boil until reduced to about 1 cup, then thicken with cornstarch or arrowroot dissolved in 1 tablespoon water. Spoon the sauce over the fish and garnish with lemon wedges.

Serves 1.

DEBRUCE STUFFING

1 teaspoon finely chopped celery
1 teaspoon finely chopped shallot
1½ teaspoons finely chopped mushrooms
½ teaspoon finely chopped onion
½ teaspoon butter
1 tablespoon white vermouth
½ teaspoon chopped fresh dill or ¼ teaspoon dried
½ teaspoon chopped fresh parsley
Salt and pepper to taste

Combine all the ingredients and mix well.

COURT-BOUILLON

4 tablespoons chopped shallots
⅓ cup dry white wine
1 teaspoon coriander
4 bay leaves
⅛ teaspoon sage
⅛ teaspoon black pepper
⅛ teaspoon paprika
⅛ teaspoon mace
Several fresh sorrel leaves
¼ cup crushed, peeled tomatoes
2 cups boiling water

Add all the ingredients to the fish poacher to flavor the trout as it cooks.

HUDSON HOUSE
Cold Spring, New York

CRISPY BROOK TROUT

Tender fish inside a crispy coating. A great way to make fish extra special.

4 to 5 whole brook trout
(8 ounces each), boned
Flour
Fritter Batter (recipe
follows)

Fat for frying
Lemon slices and fried
fresh parsley for garnish

With the trout in a butterfly configuration, dust with flour. Dip the dusted trout in the batter and immerse in heated deep fat. Cook 4-5 minutes per side or until coating is a rich, golden brown. (Note: The thick batter will slow down the cooking time.) Serve with fresh lemon slices and fried parsley. *Serves 4-5.*

FRITTER BATTER

1⅓ cups flour
Salt and pepper to taste
1 tablespoon butter,
melted
2 egg yolks, beaten
1¼ cups beer
¼ cup chopped pecans
1 tablespoon chopped
fresh parsley

1 cup Japanese bread
crumbs (or substitute
coarse, stale crumbs
from firm white bread)
2 tablespoons chopped
green onions
Pinch of dried thyme
Pinch of dried basil

In a medium bowl combine the flour, salt and pepper to taste, melted butter, and egg yolks. Mix well. Add the beer, stir, and let the mixture rest 3-12 hours. Add the pecans, parsley, bread crumbs, green onions, and herbs and mix well.

THE MANDANA INN
Skaneateles, New York

MANDANA INN BOSTON SCROD

Scrod, as you might not know, isn't a particular kind of fish but refers to any white fish that is available, usually in abundance. Here's a very simple recipe for a fresh, firm-fleshed fish, good enough to let the flavor of the fish come through.

8 ounces fresh young cod (the inn's first choice)	1 to 2 tablespoons butter, melted
½ cup coarsely crushed saltines	

Steam or poach the fish 5 minutes. Place in a baking dish, top with the crushed saltines, and drizzle with the melted butter to moisten the saltines. Broil until golden brown. *Serves 1.*

KITTLE HOUSE
Mount Kisco, New York

SWORDFISH SAUTÉ

Pernod has a strong flavor, but it goes surprisingly well with swordfish in this fine dish for a special occasion.

3 swordfish medallions	¼ cup heavy cream
(2 ounces each)	¼ cup coarsely chopped
Flour for dredging	fresh spinach
2 to 3 tablespoons	Freshly ground pepper
clarified butter	(coarse)
¼ cup Pernod	

Dredge the swordfish in flour. In a heavy skillet heat the clarified butter until hot and sauté the fish for several minutes. Drain the butter and add the Pernod. Flame. Cook over medium-high heat until the liquid in the pan is reduced by one-half. Add the cream and continue cooking until the sauce thickens. Remove from heat. Add the spinach, season with freshly ground pepper, and serve immediately.   *Serves 1.*

COLGATE INN
Hamilton, New York

SWORDFISH STEAKS
WITH CRABMEAT CRUST

A delectable way to serve swordfish. If you're on a restricted budget, try the topping with a less prized fish; just about any fish or shellfish will be enhanced by the crabmeat crust. Garnish with a bit of parsley for color.

4 swordfish steaks (about 6 ounces each), boned and skinned
2 tablespoons white wine
10 tablespoons butter, melted
6 ounces lump crabmeat
1 cup fresh bread crumbs
1½ teaspoons Worcestershire sauce
¼ cup thinly sliced scallions
2 teaspoons minced fresh basil or 1 teaspoon dried
Black pepper to taste

Arrange the steaks in a broiling pan and brush with the white wine and 2 tablespoons of the melted butter. Arrange the steaks in a flat, ovenproof dish and broil 4 minutes (keeping them about 6 inches from the heat), turn, and broil on the other side. (Broiling time will depend on the thickness of the steaks.) As the fish cooks, combine the remaining ingredients, being careful not to break up the crabmeat. Pat the crabmeat mixture on top of the cooked fish and broil until golden brown. *Serves 4.*

COUNTRY ROAD LODGE
Warrensburg, New York

QUICK AND EASY CLAM SAUCE

Makes a fine pasta course served over linguine. Or serve with garlic bread as a light main course.

1 small onion, finely
  chopped
3 cloves garlic, finely
  chopped
4 tablespoons olive oil
1 can (10 ounces) whole
  baby clams, drained
  (reserve liquid)
1 ½ tablespoons chopped
  fresh parsley

1 ½ tablespoons chopped
  fresh basil
3 tablespoons sherry
Freshly ground pepper to
  taste
½ cup buttermilk, heated
½ pound pasta, cooked
Grated Parmesan cheese

In a medium skillet sauté the onion and garlic in the oil until soft. Reduce the heat to very low and add the drained clams, parsley, and basil. Stir with a wooden spoon. Add the sherry and reserved clam juice and season with pepper. Simmer 5 minutes. Remove from the heat. Add the warm buttermilk and heat thoroughly, but do not boil. Pour over the cooked pasta. Serve with grated Parmesan cheese. *Serves 4.*

BIG MOOSE INN
Eagle Bay, New York

BAKED STUFFED CLAMS

A traditional favorite, enhanced by lemon juice. The paprika and cheese, sprinkled on just before baking, produce a lovely golden color. Fresh clams also can be used; chop them well and use all their juice.

½ cup (1 stick) butter
2 cans (6½ ounces each)
   chopped clams
Juice from 1 lemon or less
   to taste
1 medium onion, chopped
1 clove garlic, chopped
½ cup Italian-flavored
   bread crumbs

1 teaspoon dried parsley
1 teaspoon oregano
¼ teaspoon cayenne
   pepper
Grated cheddar cheese
Grated Parmesan cheese
Paprika

In a medium saucepan melt the butter and add the clams, lemon juice, onion, and garlic. Simmer 15 minutes, stirring occasionally. In a small bowl combine the bread crumbs, parsley, oregano, and cayenne pepper. Stir the crumb mixture into the clam mixture in the pan. Preheat oven to 400°F. Fill 8 clam shells or small casserole dishes with the clam mixture. Sprinkle with the grated cheese and paprika. Bake 10 minutes or until bubbly and brown.   *Serves 8.*

ROUNDUP RANCH
Downsville, New York

SHRIMP CASSEROLE

A tasty blend of shrimp, crabmeat, and vegetables in a rich, creamy sauce. Betty Gunn, who developed this recipe, prepares it for a crowd and bakes it as a casserole. For 4-6, it works better when served in individual gratinée dishes.

½ green pepper, chopped	1 to 2 hard-boiled eggs,
1 celery stalk, chopped	thickly sliced
½ medium onion,	1½ tablespoons butter
chopped	1½ tablespoons flour
1 cup water	1 cup light cream
2 to 4 tablespoons	½ cup shredded sharp
chopped pimiento	cheddar cheese
¼ pound crabmeat	Salt and pepper to taste
½ pound shrimp, cleaned,	½ cup buttered bread
deveined, and cooked	crumbs

In a medium saucepan combine the pepper, celery, onion, and water and cook until the vegetables are tender. Drain. Add the pimiento, crabmeat, shrimp, and eggs. Set aside. In a second saucepan melt the butter. Sprinkle in the flour and cook, stirring constantly, for several minutes. Gradually add the cream and cook, stirring constantly, until the mixture thickens. Add the cheese and salt and pepper to taste. Preheat oven to 400°F. Pour the sauce over the shrimp mixture and stir until well blended. Spoon the mixture into individual gratinée dishes. Sprinkle the bread crumbs over the top and bake 15-20 minutes. *Serves 4-6.*

GIDEON PUTNAM
Saratoga Springs, New York

CHEF OTTO'S SHRIMP
IN WINE AND CREAM SAUCE

Tender shrimp in a delectable sauce. Serve with a lightly sautéed vegetable.

10 large shrimp, peeled
  and deveined
Flour seasoned to taste
  with salt and pepper for
  dredging
3 tablespoons butter
1 teaspoon minced shallot

1 cup sliced mushrooms
½ cup dry white wine
½ cup heavy cream
Salt and pepper to taste
½ teaspoon chopped fresh
  parsley

Dredge the shrimp in seasoned flour. In a heavy skillet or sauté pan heat the butter and sauté the shrimp over medium heat about 1 minute, turning to brown both sides. Add the shallots and mushrooms and cook 2-3 minutes more. Add the wine and cook until reduced by one-half. Add the heavy cream, bring to a boil, and cook until slightly thickened. Season with salt and pepper. Serve immediately, sprinkled with chopped parsley.

Serves 2.

SNAPPER INN
Oakdale, New York

SHRIMP BELVEDERE

Use the largest shrimp you can find for the best results. This dish also can be served as an appetizer. To butterfly a shrimp, cut along the underside to the depth of the vein.

1 cup bread crumbs	15 strips bacon
1 cup Parmesan cheese	30 large shrimp, peeled,
½ cup chopped fresh	deveined, and
parsley	butterflied
1 tablespoon oregano	
¼ pound Swiss cheese,	
sliced	

Preheat oven to 450°F. In a shallow bowl combine the bread crumbs, Parmesan cheese, parsley, and oregano. Cut the Swiss cheese slices into strips the length of the shrimp, about ⅛ inch thick. Cut the bacon strips in half. Place 1 strip of Swiss cheese on each shrimp, fold closed, and wrap with bacon. Roll the shrimp in the bread crumb mixture. Arrange in a shallow baking dish and bake 10 minutes. Broil 1 minute longer on each side to crisp the bacon. *Serves 6.*

BIG MOOSE INN
Eagle Bay, New York

SEAFOOD BISQUE

Absolutely delicious. Use equal amounts of the three kinds of seafood recommended or make this dish with just one main ingredient.

7 tablespoons butter	10 tablespoons sherry
½ pound shrimp, scallops, and crabmeat	Salt and pepper to taste
1 tablespoon chopped shallot or 2 tablespoons chopped onion	3 tablespoons flour
	1½ cups milk
	Seasoned bread crumbs
	Grated Parmesan cheese

Preheat oven to 400°F. In a heavy skillet melt 4 tablespoons of the butter and sauté the shrimp, scallops, crabmeat, and shallot or onion for 5 minutes. Sprinkle with 6 tablespoons of the sherry and season with salt and pepper. In another saucepan melt the remaining 3 tablespoons butter and slowly stir in the flour. Cook several minutes over low heat. Add the milk and remaining 4 tablespoons sherry, stirring constantly, until mixture is smooth. Combine the sauce and seafood in a buttered 1-quart casserole dish. Cover the top with the seasoned bread crumbs and sprinkle with cheese. Bake 30 minutes.

Serves 4.

SNAPPER INN
Oakdale, New York

SHRIMP DIANE

Rich and flavorful, a special dish to serve with a combination of red and green vegetables. The inn recommends spooning it over rice.

1¾ pounds medium
  shrimp
Shrimp Stock (recipe
  follows)
¼ cup butter
¼ cup finely diced
  scallions
½ teaspoon cayenne
  pepper
¼ teaspoon white pepper
¼ teaspoon black pepper

½ teaspoon minced garlic
Salt to taste
¼ teaspoon basil
¼ teaspoon thyme
¼ teaspoon oregano
½ pound mushrooms,
  sliced
6 ounces heavy cream
¼ cup chopped fresh
  parsley

Peel, devein, and butterfly the shrimp. Set the peels aside to make the Shrimp Stock. Melt the butter in a large skillet. Sauté the shrimp for several minutes until barely cooked. Set aside. Add the scallions, pepper, garlic, salt, basil, thyme, and oregano. Cook 1 minute, stirring constantly. Add the mushrooms and Shrimp Stock and cook 1 minute longer. Add the heavy cream and cook 3-5 minutes until reduced to the consistency of a sauce. Add the shrimp and heat through. Remove from heat, stir in the parsley, and serve.   *Serves 4.*

SHRIMP STOCK

Peels from shrimp (see
  previous recipe)
¼ cup chopped carrots
¼ cup chopped celery
¼ cup chopped onions
¼ cup chopped tomatoes

½ teaspoon celery salt
½ teaspoon black pepper
½ teaspoon onion powder
½ teaspoon garlic powder
2 cups cold water

Combine all the ingredients in a heavy kettle. Bring to a boil, reduce heat, and simmer 30 minutes. Strain.

GENESEE FALLS INN
Portageville, New York

BAY SCALLOPS EN CASSEROLE

A very easy dish to put together, best made with tiny, fresh scallops. Serve over rice (the inn uses individual casseroles) and accompany with a green salad.

2 tablespoons butter
¾ pound bay scallops
½ to 1 teaspoon chopped
  fresh garlic

Dash of white port
Chopped parsley

In a medium saucepan heat the butter. Sauté the scallops in the butter for 2-3 minutes. Add the remaining ingredients, and cook over low heat until the scallops are tender and heated through, approximately 3-4 minutes. (Be careful not to overcook, or the scallops will become tough.)   *Serves 2.*

LE CHAMBORD
Hopewell Junction, New York

COQUILLES ST. JACQUES HENRY

An unusual combination of ingredients results in a fine contrast of color and flavor. When you make this dish and taste it, you'll appreciate the creativity of executive chef Henry-Paul. If you can't find bilberry jelly, substitute currant or blueberry.

1 pound sea scallops
Flour for dredging
  (seasoned to taste with
  garlic powder, dried
  oregano, paprika, salt,
  and pepper)
2 to 4 tablespoons
  clarified butter
¾ cup port
Thinly sliced peel and
  juice from ½ orange

Thinly sliced peel and
  juice from ½ lemon
1 shallot, chopped
½ teaspoon Dijon
  mustard
½ teaspoon thinly sliced
  fresh ginger
Dash of Tabasco
1 teaspoon bilberry jelly
2 tablespoons glace of fish
3 tablespoons butter

Dredge the scallops in seasoned flour and shake off excess flour. Heat the clarified butter until hot and sauté the scallops for several minutes, turning to brown evenly. Remove to a hot platter. In a saucepan combine the port, orange and lemon peels, and orange and lemon juice. Cook over medium heat until reduced by about one-half. Add the shallot, mustard, ginger, and Tabasco and reduce again. Add the jelly, glace, and butter. Heat and spoon over the scallops. *Serves 4.*

PARTRIDGE BERRY INN
Watertown, New York

CURRIED SCALLOPS

Scallops go extremely well with this full-flavored curry sauce.

½ cup (1 stick) butter
½ cup finely chopped onion
½ cup finely chopped celery
1 medium apple, peeled, cored, and chopped
1 teaspoon minced fresh parsley
1 clove garlic, minced
½ bay leaf
⅛ teaspoon dry mustard

2 tablespoons flour
¼ teaspoon mace
1 tablespoon curry powder
¾ cup clam broth
½ cup white wine
1½ pounds scallops
¼ cup heavy cream
Toasted coconut and chopped peanuts for garnish

Melt the butter in a heavy skillet. Add the onion, celery, and apple and sauté until soft. Add the minced parsley and garlic. Add the bay leaf and dry mustard and sauté 8 minutes. Add the flour, mace, and curry powder and sauté 4 minutes. Stir in the clam broth and white wine and simmer 45 minutes. Remove the bay leaf. Add the scallops and simmer 10 minutes. Add the cream and heat just enough to warm thoroughly. Do not boil. Serve topped with toasted coconut and peanuts. *Serves 4-6.*

HUDSON HOUSE
Cold Spring, New York

SCALLOPS HUDSON HOUSE

Pernod gives this dish a strong but delightful flavor. For non-licorice (anise) lovers, use framboise or Cointreau.

6 tablespoons vegetable oil	3 ounces mushrooms, cut
½ pound sea scallops	into quarters
Flour for dredging	½ cup fresh spinach
3 tablespoons Pernod	leaves, finely sliced
6 tablespoons heavy	Salt and pepper to taste
cream	

In a heavy skillet heat the oil until smoking. Dredge the scallops in flour and shake off any excess. Brown the scallops on both sides in the hot oil. Remove from the pan and pour off the excess oil. Return the pan to the heat. Add the Pernod, heavy cream, and mushrooms and cook 2-3 minutes or until the mushrooms are almost tender and the cream is reduced by about one-half. Add the spinach and scallops and season with salt and pepper. Heat thoroughly. *Serves 2.*

BEEF AND VEAL

GOLD MOUNTAIN CHALET
Spring Glen, New York

BEEF-BROCCOLI PIE

A rich and filling one-dish meal that provides a tasty way to get children to eat their broccoli. The inn recommends using a cake pan rather than a pie tin to hold all the filling.

1 pound ground beef	1½ teaspoons salt
1 onion, chopped	½ teaspoon pepper
1 clove garlic	8 ounces Monterey Jack
1 package (3 ounces)	cheese
cream cheese	Pastry for one 2-crust, 9-
1 cup chopped broccoli	inch pie
2 eggs	

Preheat oven to 350°F. In a heavy skillet sauté the ground beef, onion, and garlic until the meat is browned. Add the cream cheese and stir until the cheese melts and coats the other ingredients. Stir in the broccoli. Beat in the eggs and season with salt and pepper. Line the bottom of the pie shell with half the Monterey Jack cheese. Fill the shell with the beef and broccoli mixture. Sprinkle the remaining cheese on top. Cover with the top crust. Bake 1 hour.   *Serves 6.*

AUBERGE DES 4 SAISONS
Shandaken, New York

BOEUF AUX CAROTTES

This recipe calls for larding the beef, a process that enriches the meat but has gone out of vogue lately. That step can be omitted, but you won't be preparing this dish the way the inn does. A calf's foot or several pigs' feet added to the simmering liquid in the first hour will greatly enhance the sauce. Serve with crusty French bread.

¼ pound hard back fat (optional)
1 clove garlic, chopped
¼ bunch parsley
Salt and pepper to taste
1 bottom round (3 to 4 pounds)
2 tablespoons fat or butter
4 medium onions, sliced
¼ cup cognac
3 ripe tomatoes, peeled, seeded, and chopped (or use canned whole tomatoes)

1 bottle dry white wine
Beef stock
1 bouquet garni (ideally made up of leek greens, parsley with the root, thyme, bay leaf, marjoram, and lovage)
2 tablespoons lard or rendered drippings
4 tablespoons flour
1 bunch carrots
1 tablespoon butter

Cut the back fat into ¼-inch-square lardons as long as the meat. (This is much easier if the back fat is very cold. Put it in the freezer for 10-20 minutes.) Toss the fat with the garlic, parsley, and salt and pepper to taste. With a larding needle lard the meat in a decorative pattern and tie it up neatly with kitchen string. In a deep kettle or Dutch oven heat the 2 tablespoons fat or butter and brown the meat on all sides. Remove the meat. Add the sliced onions and brown them. Add the cognac and flame. Then add the tomatoes. Return the meat to the pan. Add enough wine to cover about two-thirds of the meat. Then add enough beef stock to cover the meat. Add the bouquet garni and simmer, covered, over very low heat for 4 hours. Remove the meat to a heated platter and keep warm. Melt the lard or drippings in a heavy pan, sprinkle in the flour, and stir over medium heat until brown. Strain the stock into the browned flour, stirring with a whisk to form a smooth sauce. Reduce the stock by one-third or until it coats a spoon. As the sauce reduces, skim the surface. Season to taste with salt and pepper.

As the sauce cooks down, peel and quarter the carrots. Cut them into 1-inch lengths. Cook them in boiling salted water until tender but still crispy. Drain and toss in the butter. Slice the meat and transfer it to a hot serving platter. Surround with plenty of sauce and mounds of carrots. Pass any extra sauce around in a sauce boat. *Serves 6-8.*

THE ALGONQUIN
New York, New York

MARINATED BEEF

Start the preparations for this dish several days in advance and don't cheat on the marinating time. Noodles or mashed potatoes are fine companions to this old favorite.

4 to 5 pounds beef (round or rump)	1 bay leaf
½ pound salt pork	¼ cup chopped onion
1 teaspoon each cloves, allspice, thyme, and pepper	¼ cup chopped fresh parsley
1½ cups mild vinegar	Fat or butter
	1 cup water

Wipe the meat with a damp cloth and remove any uneven trimmings and fat. Cut the salt pork into long strips, ¼-inch wide. Mix the spices and roll the pork strips in the mixture until evenly coated. Cut gashes in the beef, insert the seasoned pork strips (or put them in with a larding needle), and place the meat in a deep bowl. Bring the vinegar to a boil and add the bay leaf, onion, and parsley. Cool and pour over the meat. Place the bowl in the refrigerator and turn the meat often during this "pickling" period. After three days remove the meat, wipe dry, place in a heavy kettle or Dutch oven, and sear in hot fat or butter. Strain the marinade. Add 1 cup marinade and 1 cup water to the Dutch oven and simmer gently, covered, 3 hours or until tender. *Serves 10-12.*

Sauce for Beef (Optional): Remove the meat after cooking and keep warm. Add any remaining marinade plus ½ cup vinegar to the liquid in the pan, along with 2 to 3 tablespoons sugar. Bring to a boil, reduce heat, and thicken with 1 tablespoon cornstarch. Serve over the meat.

THE ALGONQUIN
New York, New York

HUNGARIAN BEEF STEW

This recipe, featured in the inn's cookbook, Feeding the Lions, *has long been a favorite item on the menu. Serve with noodles, preferably homemade. For additional flavor add caraway seeds, paprika, chopped tomatoes and sweet peppers, and minced garlic to taste.*

1 cup (2 sticks) butter or drippings	1½ teaspoons salt
	1½ teaspoons paprika
3 pounds beef chuck or shoulder cut in 1½-inch slices	1 cup flour
	1 cup tomato purée
1 bay leaf	1 quart water or beef stock
3 large onions, sliced	

In a heavy casserole or Dutch oven melt the butter (or heat the drippings), add the beef and bay leaf, sprinkle with the onions and salt, and simmer until golden brown. Combine the paprika and flour and stir into the tomato purée and water or stock. Remove the meat from the pan and add the tomato mixture. Stir to incorporate any bits from the pan. Return the meat to the pan and cook slowly, either on top of the stove or in a 300°F. oven for 1½-2 hours or until meat is tender.   *Serves 8-10.*

PLEASANT VIEW LODGE
Freehold, New York

SAUERBRATEN

An authentic German dish with slightly tart beef and a sweet-and-sour gravy. The beef requires a week to marinate, so this entrée definitely requires advance planning. By varying the amounts of sugar, vinegar, and water in the marinade, you can control the intensity of the flavor and adjust it to your own taste. In German tradition the best accompaniments would be red cabbage and spaetzle or potato pancakes. Both the meat and the gravy freeze well, so it pays to prepare a large amount.

4 pounds bottom round
1½ cups white vinegar
1½ cups wine vinegar
1½ cups water
Generous pinch of
   pickling spice
¾ teaspoon salt
¼ teaspoon pepper
2½ tablespoons sugar
2½ teaspoons soy sauce
½ teaspoon Worcestershire
   sauce
Dash of Tabasco

2½ teaspoons monosodium
   glutamate (optional)
3 stalks celery, chopped
½ large Spanish onion
2 cloves garlic, chopped
5 tablespoons butter
5 tablespoons flour
2½ cups beef stock
6 to 8 ginger snaps,
   crushed
2 tablespoons cornstarch
2 tablespoons water

Trim all the fat and silverskin from the bottom round. Combine the vinegars, 1½ cups water, pickling spice, salt, pepper, sugar, soy sauce, Worcestershire sauce, Tabasco, monosodium glutamate (if used), celery, onion, and garlic. Marinate the meat for 1 week. (A heavy-duty plastic bag will work well.)

To cook, preheat oven to 325°F. and roast the meat approximately 1 hour 20 minutes or until it reaches an internal temperature of 120°F. As the meat cooks, pour the marinade into a large pot and bring it to a boil. Add the roasted meat and simmer until it reaches an internal temperature of 140°F. Add the butter to the drippings in the pan and stir until it melts. Sprinkle in the flour and cook over low heat, stirring constantly, until smooth. Add the beef stock and continue cooking and stirring to create a smooth gravy. Remove the beef from the marinade and set aside. Add the ginger snaps and gravy to the marinade. Combine the cornstarch and 2 tablespoons water to form a smooth paste and stir into the liquid. Taste and adjust the seasonings. Simmer 20 minutes. Strain and discard the vegetables. Slice the beef in ¼-inch-thick slices and serve with a generous portion of gravy. *Serves 8.*

THE CONCORD
Kiamesha Lake, New York

SWEET-AND-SOUR STUFFED CABBAGE

Tightly wrapped rolls of beef and veal, covered in cabbage and simmered in a sweet-and-sour sauce. To make the sauce more piquant, add a dash of vinegar. Serve over rice as a hearty main course or slice and serve as an appetizer.

Water	2 eggs, beaten
4½ pounds cabbage	Salt and pepper to taste
1½ pounds ground beef and veal	Marinade (recipe follows)
1 large onion, minced	Sweet-and-Sour Sauce (recipe follows)
1½ tablespoons sugar	

Fill a large kettle half full of water, bring to a boil, drop in the cabbage, and boil 10 minutes. Keeping the water at a boil, carefully lift out the cabbage, pull off all the outer leaves that are loose, and return the tight inner head to the kettle. Boil, remove, and pull off leaves several times until you have about 26 leaves. In a medium bowl combine the ground beef and veal, minced onion, sugar, eggs, and salt and pepper to taste. Mix well. Place the parboiled cabbage leaves on a flat surface. Spoon approximately 2 tablespoons of the meat mixture onto the center of each leaf and roll tightly, tucking in the ends. Arrange the cabbage rolls in the bottom of a 4-quart casserole or Dutch oven. Pour the marinade over them and bring to a boil. Reduce the heat, cover tightly, and simmer 1-1½ hours or until the cabbage is tender. Serve hot, with sauce. *Serves 6-8.*

MARINADE

2 tablespoons butter
1 large onion, diced
2 large meaty bones
1 large apple, peeled and
  sliced

½ cup raisins
½ cup crushed pineapple
1 quart beef or veal stock

In a large skillet or kettle melt the butter and sauté the onion until soft. Add the bones and brown on all sides. Add the apple, raisins, pineapple, and stock. Simmer 1 hour. Strain.

SWEET-AND-SOUR SAUCE

3 cans (16 to 17 ounces
  each) tomato sauce
4 tablespoons brown
  sugar

Juice of 2 lemons
Salt and pepper to taste

In a heavy saucepan combine all the ingredients, bring to a boil, reduce the heat, and simmer several minutes.

THE OTESAGA AND COOPER INN
Cooperstown, New York

BEEF AND PORK BROCHETTE WITH HONEY GLAZE

Use naturally tender meat for the best results from this tasty dish. Do not thread beef and pork on the same skewer unless you want your beef very well done. Serve over rice.

1 pound lean, tender beef, cubed

1 pound lean, tender pork, cubed

⅔ pound mushroom caps

⅔ pound red or green peppers, cut in 1½-inch strips

⅔ pound onions, cut in 1½-inch strips

⅔ pound tomatoes, cut in wedges (or use cherry tomatoes, whole)

10 tablespoons honey

2 tablespoons lemon juice

Alternately thread meat and vegetables on skewers, putting beef and pork on separate skewers. Mix the honey with the lemon juice and brush on the brochettes. Broil in the oven or over hot coals, turning and basting with glaze several times, until the beef is cooked to taste and the pork is well done, approximately 10 minutes for the beef, 15-20 minutes for the pork, depending on the size of the cubes and the method of cooking. *Serves 4-6.*

GENEVA ON THE LAKE
Geneva, New York

VEAL SCAMPI DIANNE

This combination of veal and shrimp in a rich and zesty sauce is easy to prepare and guarantees impressive results and generous servings. Rice pilaf is a fine accompaniment.

Flour for dredging	¼ cup sliced mushrooms
Salt and pepper to taste	¼ cup heavy cream
6 ounces veal scallops, pounded thin and cut into 3 pieces	2 tablespoons Dijon mustard
4 tablespoons butter	2 tablespoons minced shallots
3 jumbo raw shrimp, cleaned and deveined	6 drops Worcestershire sauce
2 tablespoons brandy	

Season the flour with salt and pepper. Dredge the veal in the flour. Melt the butter in a heavy skillet and sauté the veal on both sides. Remove to a warm platter. Sauté the shrimp in the same pan and arrange them on top of the veal with their tails up. Pour the brandy into the pan, flame, and deglaze the pan. Add the remaining ingredients and cook over medium heat until the sauce is reduced by one-third. Pour the sauce over the shrimp and veal and serve.   *Serves 1.*

AUBERGE DES 4 SAISONS
Shandaken, New York

ROGNON DE VEAU À L'ANCIENNE

"This method of preparing veal kidneys should please even the most wary," innkeeper Tim Knab says. *"It eliminates the acrid taste that most people object to in kidneys. All of our menus are in French, and every so often an unknowing diner will order this dish without realizing that it's a kidney. Invariably there are compliments, sometimes accompanied by a puzzled look when the diner is informed of what he or she has just eaten!"* Serve this dish with rice pilaf and a vegetable. A small amount of meat glaze added to the sauce with the cognac will enhance the flavor.

4 fresh veal kidneys
4 tablespoons peanut oil
1 tablespoon butter
2 shallots, chopped
1 teaspoon Dijon mustard
¼ cup cognac
1 cup heavy cream

Salt and pepper to taste
½ pound mushrooms, sliced and sautéed in butter
¼ pound fresh or frozen pearl onions, boiled

Peel away the outer membrane from the kidneys and pare out the fat from the center. Cut the kidneys into ¼-inch-thick slices about 1 inch wide. In a large, heavy skillet heat 1 tablespoon of the peanut oil until hot. Over high heat toss the first sliced kidney into the pan for not more than 1 minute. Remove it to a large colander and let drain. Repeat this procedure with each remaining kidney. (Cooking the kidneys quickly in very hot oil causes them to contract and exude much of their juice, which contains the acrid taste.) Drain the pan. Keep the kidneys in a warm place while preparing the sauce.

Add the butter and chopped shallots to the sauté pan and cook over medium heat. When the shallots just begin to brown, add the mustard and then the cognac. Allow all the cognac to cook down, then add the cream. Reduce until the cream begins to thicken and correct the seasoning. Add the mushrooms and onions. Discard the liquid from the kidneys and add the kidneys to the sauce just long enough to reheat them. Do not allow the sauce to boil, or the kidneys will toughen.   *Serves 2-4.*

BEEKMAN ARMS
Rhinebeck, New York

VEAL BEEKMAN

Celebrate a special occasion with this beautiful dish that combines the strong taste of sun-dried tomatoes and the subtle flavor of rosemary. Purchase the tomatoes dry, reconstitute them in white wine, and marinate them in olive oil with fresh garlic and basil. Or buy them in oil and drain well.

2 to 3 cups Brown Sauce
  (recipe follows)
2 tablespoons tomato
  purée
1 sachet bag containing ¼
  bay leaf, a pinch of
  rosemary, 3 crushed
  black peppercorns, and
  1 clove garlic
8 large mushrooms, sliced
½ cup beef stock

Flour for dredging
Salt and pepper to taste
4 veal cutlets (about 4
  ounces each), pounded
  thin
2 tablespoons butter
2 ounces prosciutto,
  julienned
4 ounces sun-dried
  tomatoes, julienned

In a large saucepan combine the Brown Sauce and tomato purée, add the sachet bag, and simmer 10-15 minutes or until you can taste the rosemary in the sauce. Strain the sauce and remove the sachet bag. Simmer the mushrooms in the beef stock, drain, and set aside. Season the flour with salt and pepper and dredge the veal; shake off any excess flour. Melt the butter in a skillet and sauté the veal quickly over high heat, turning to brown both sides. Remove the veal to a warm plate. Pour the sauce into the skillet and deglaze the pan by stirring until smooth. Bring the sauce to a simmer and return the veal to the skillet to reheat. To present, arrange the veal on a serving platter in a shingled fashion. Pour about ½ cup of sauce over the veal and garnish with the sliced mushrooms and the julienne of prosciutto and dried tomatoes.

Serves 4.

BROWN SAUCE

This versatile sauce depends on the flavor of browned butter. Watch it carefully — there's a thin line between browned and burned! Beekman Arms uses large quantities made according to institutional menu needs. The following basic recipe will work for the home cook. Flavor the sauce with an onion and herbs if desired. See Chasseur Brown Sauce (page 211) for another variation.

¼ cup butter	Salt and pepper to taste
¼ cup flour	2 cups veal or beef stock

In a heavy saucepan melt the butter. Cook over low heat until the butter begins to brown. Sprinkle in the flour and salt and pepper to taste and cook, stirring occasionally, for several minutes, until the flour turns brown. Slowly add the veal or beef stock, stirring constantly, until the sauce is smooth. Bring to a boil, reduce heat, and simmer 10 minutes.   *Makes 2 cups.*

THE HORNED DORSET
Leonardsville, New York

VEAL CHASSEUR

An elegant, classic dish using wild mushrooms that goes well with colorful vegetables such as broccoli and carrots. The inn serves it with wild rice.

1 loin of veal, boned and sliced into 4-ounce portions	2 cups Chasseur Brown Sauce (recipe follows)
2 to 3 tablespoons butter	1 tomato, seeded and chopped
3 large shallots or 1 onion, chopped	Salt and white pepper to taste
2 ounces dried cèpes, soaked in ¾ cup water	Worcestershire sauce to taste
¾ cup dry white wine	

Cut each piece of veal cross-grain and pound to form thin medallions. In a large frying pan sauté the veal in about 2 tablespoons of the butter over high heat for several minutes per side. Remove the veal from the pan and keep warm. Saute the shallots or onion in the remaining butter until soft. Add the cèpes and their soaking liquid, the white wine, and the Chasseur Brown Sauce. Simmer 10 minutes. Then add the tomato, salt and pepper, and Worcestershire sauce. Simmer until the liquid is reduced by one-third. Skim and correct the seasoning. Warm the veal in the sauce and serve. *Serves 6.*

CHASSEUR BROWN SAUCE

Not all brown sauces are the same. Here's another variation, as prepared at the inn.

6 tablespoons butter	4 cups brown stock
¼ cup flour	1 bay leaf
1 onion, coarsely chopped	1 tablespoon fresh thyme
2 carrots, coarsely chopped	

In a heavy saucepan melt the butter and brown the flour over low heat. Add the onion and carrots and sauté until brown, stirring constantly. Stir in the stock, add the bay leaf and thyme, and simmer 1 hour. Stir occasionally throughout the cooking to prevent sticking. Skim and strain, retaining the liquid.

LANZA'S COUNTRY INN
Livingston Manor, New York

VEAL LOMBARDO

Make this dish at the last minute, and no one will ever know you didn't labor over it for hours. The flavor is enhanced with beef base, a product sold by restaurant supply stores. You can easily increase the amounts for multiple servings; sauté the veal in batches. The inn serves this with fresh pasta.

1 veal cutlet (4 to 6 ounces), pounded thin	⅛ teaspoon beef base
Flour for dredging	3 to 4 fresh basil leaves
1 to 2 tablespoons olive oil	¼ cup white wine
⅛ teaspoon chopped garlic	½ cup chunky tomato sauce

Dredge the veal in flour and shake off any excess. In a heavy skillet heat the oil until hot and sauté the veal until brown on both sides. Remove to a warm plate. Add the remaining ingredients to the skillet and simmer 1 minute, stirring to blend well. Pour over warm veal. *Serves 1.*

YE HARE 'N HOUNDS INN
Bemus Point, New York

VEAL SAINT PHILLIPE

A good main dish for a festive occasion. Slice the lemon very thin so it doesn't overpower the subtle flavors of the other ingredients. The inn uses an institutional au jus base to make this dish; we have substituted stock, which the home cook is more likely to have on hand.

4 veal medallions, pounded thin	2 large mushroom caps
Flour for dredging	2 artichoke hearts
3 tablespoons butter	1 tablespoon sliced almonds
½ cup chicken or veal stock	Dash of golden sherry
	½ lemon, thinly sliced

Dredge the veal in flour. Melt the butter in a heavy, shallow pan and gently sauté the veal for several minutes on both sides. (If your pan isn't large enough to accommodate all the veal at once, sauté it in batches and return all the veal to the pan before continuing with the recipe.) Add the chicken or veal stock, mushroom caps, artichoke hearts, almonds, and sherry and simmer 10 minutes. Add the lemon slices and simmer 1 minute longer. Serve immediately. *Serves 2.*

TROUTBECK
Amenia, New York

VEAL PÊCHE

Simple to make and elegant to serve. The peach slices are an intriguing and appetizing touch that departs from more traditional ways of preparing veal.

4 ounces veal, pounded
  very thin
Flour for dredging
1 egg, beaten
Bread crumbs (preferably
  from French loaves)
2 tablespoons clarified
  butter
½ shallot, minced

¼ cup Madeira
Pinch of freshly ground
  black pepper
  (preferably from
  tellicherry peppercorns)
1 ripe peach, peeled and
  sliced
¼ cup heavy cream

Dredge the veal in flour, dip it in the beaten egg, and roll it in the bread crumbs. Heat the clarified butter until hot and sauté the veal, turning quickly. Remove the veal to a warm plate. Add the shallot and Madeira to the pan and flame. Add the pepper and peach slices and reduce the liquid in the pan by two-thirds. Add the cream and reduce again until the sauce is thick. Arrange the peach slices around the veal and spoon the sauce on top.

Serves 1.

KITTLE HOUSE
Mount Kisco, New York

ESCALOPES OF VEAL

Another quick but elegant veal entrée. If fresh fennel is not available, grind a pinch of fennel seeds with a mortar and pestle; they will be stronger than the fresh herb.

2 veal medallions (2 ounces each), pounded very thin	1 shallot, diced
	1 tablespoon fresh fennel
Flour for dredging	¼ cup Madeira
2 tablespoons clarified butter	¼ cup Brown Sauce (see recipes on pages 209 and 211)

Dredge the veal in flour. Melt the clarified butter in a skillet until hot. Sauté the veal on both sides and remove to a warm plate. Add the shallot, fennel, Madeira, and Brown Sauce to the juice in the pan. Cook over medium heat until the sauce is reduced by about one-half. Spoon over the veal and serve immediately.   *Serves 1.*

PORK AND LAMB

BIG MOOSE INN
Eagle Bay, New York

BROILED PORK CHOP MARINADE

A sweet and slightly spicy marinade, enough to flavor 6 pork chops. The inn serves its marinated chops on a bed of rice and sprinkles them with chopped parsley. Any drippings from the pan are spooned over the rice.

½ cup brown sugar
¼ cup cider vinegar
1 tablespoon brown mustard
1 teaspoon Worcestershire sauce

Dash of ground cloves
Dash of marjoram
6 pork chops

Combine all the ingredients except the pork chops in a glass or coated enamel bowl. Place the pork chops in the marinade and let sit at least 3 hours at room temperature. Broil 20-30 minutes, turning once, depending on the thickness of the chops. *Serves 3-6.*

THE OLD DUTCH INN
Kinderhook, New York

MARINADE FOR LAMB

A good bit of this marinade, which the inn calls its "Sauce Piquante," clings to the lamb as it cooks, creating an even coating of herbs and a lovely brown color. The inn uses this recipe for individual lamb roasts; it also works well with lamb chops and pork chops. Use 2 cups of your favorite vinaigrette dressing as the base and add the fennel seeds and anchovies, or make everything from scratch.

9 tablespoons red wine vinegar
1 tablespoon chopped garlic
6 tablespoons Dijon mustard
1½ teaspoons dried oregano
1 tablespoon ground cumin
1¾ cups olive oil
1 teaspoon crushed fennel seed
6 anchovy fillets, chopped

In a glass or nonmetallic bowl combine all the ingredients and blend well. Pour over the lamb and marinate 2-3 days in the refrigerator. *Makes 2 cups.*

TAVERN ON THE GREEN
New York, New York

SAUTÉED LAMB LOIN

A mouth-watering combination of sautéed vegetables, topped with tender, succulent slices of lamb, this elegant dish is surprisingly easy to prepare. The restaurant uses truffle juice to enhance its brown sauce. With an eye toward cooks with more modest pantry stock, we suggest Madeira to make the sauce a bit tastier.

1 to 3 tablespoons butter
½ medium shallot
1 clove garlic
½ cup diced tomatoes
Salt and pepper to taste
3 medium mushrooms, sliced
½ cup chopped fresh spinach
1 lamb loin (4½ ounces), cleaned and trimmed

Oil for cooking
⅓ cup Brown Sauce (see pages 209 and 211)
1 tablespoon Madeira
2 tablespoons tomato concasse*
Chopped fresh herbs for garnish

Melt ⅓ of the butter in a small skillet and sauté the shallot and garlic until soft. Add the diced tomatoes and cook for several minutes over low heat, until the tomatoes soften. Season to taste with salt and pepper. Melt another ⅓ of the butter in a second skillet and sauté the mushrooms until soft. Add the tomato mixture and stir until blended. In the first skillet melt the remaining butter and sauté the spinach until tender. Remove from the skillet and add to the tomato mixture. Spoon the mixture onto a plate and press it down to form a bed for the lamb loin. Keep warm.

Preheat oven to 500°F. Season the loin with salt and pepper, sear it in hot oil, and bake it in the oven until medium rare. Let sit 15-20 minutes. Cut into thin slices and arrange over the bed of vegetables. Heat the Brown Sauce and stir in the Madeira. Spoon the concasse over the lamb, top with the warm sauce, and garnish with a sprinkling of herbs.   *Serves 1.*

*To prepare a concasse, peel, halve, and seed a fresh tomato; then roughly chop or coarsely shred it.

DEPUY CANAL HOUSE
High Falls, New York

ORANGE LAMB SKIRTS WITH SAUSAGE STUFFING

Chef John Novi developed this recipe and has this to say about it: *"Lamb skirts are rarely used in cooking, and while they are relatively inexpensive when compared to other pieces of lamb, they might be a bit difficult to get, due to the butchering involved. If you are considering doing a number of lamb dishes, order a saddle of lamb and ask your butcher to separate the parts. One of the reasons I enjoy using lamb skirts is that they can be used as a wrapping for any number of stuffings: chicken purée, veal mousse, or venison."* This dish presents handsome rounds of lamb filled with a savory sausage stuffing and topped with a sweet-tart citrus sauce. Serve with rice and a green vegetable.

1 lamb loin with skirt	1 onion, sliced
Sausage Stuffing (recipe follows)	½ cup white wine
Freshly ground pepper	Orange Sauce (recipe follows)

Preheat oven to 400°F. Remove any excess fat on the lamb skirt. Spread the skirt out flat, skin side down, and place a mound of Sausage Stuffing on the skirt, leaning against the loin meat and extending the length of the loin. Place the roll into a butcher's net. (This can be tricky, so you might want to use a metal #10 coffee can as a guide; cut out the top and bottom, stretch the mesh net over one end, and push the rolled skirt through from the other end. As it comes through, the mesh will wrap around it.) If netting cannot be obtained, tie the lamb well with kitchen twine. Once tied, roll the skirt in freshly ground pepper. Place in a hot pan and sear over high heat. Remove to a roasting pan, place sliced onion over the skirt, fill the pan one-quarter full of water, and add the wine. Bake ½ hour or to desired doneness (120°F. for rare, 150°F. for medium). Remove from the oven and let cool. Prior to serving, slice the lamb skirts into 1-inch-thick slices and top with the Orange Sauce. Return the slices to the oven at 400°F. until the Orange Sauce becomes a glaze and the slices are thoroughly heated.

Serves 8-10.

SAUSAGE STUFFING

6 links sweet Italian sausage
1 ½ cups cubed stale bread, soaked in warm water and squeezed dry

2 tablespoons chopped fresh parsley
3 eggs
Salt and pepper to taste

Remove the sausage from the casing and cook in a heavy skillet, chopping it into small pieces as it cooks. Drain well. Place in a bowl along with the moist, compact bread. Add the parsley, eggs, and salt and pepper to taste. With an open hand mix until well blended.

ORANGE SAUCE

1 cup water
Peel from 2 lemons and 2 oranges

¾ cup sugar
4 oranges, peeled and sliced

In a heavy saucepan combine the water, peel, and sugar. Bring to a boil and cook until the syrup thickens slightly. Place the oranges in a deep glass dish and pour the syrup over them. Use one orange slice to garnish each slice of lamb skirt.

HUDSON HOUSE
Cold Spring, New York

PERSIAN PLEASURE

This hearty fare makes a good cold-weather meal. Serve with rice pilaf and garnish each dish with fresh mint.

2 medium eggplants
Salt
2 tablespoons olive oil
1 medium onion, diced
2 cloves garlic, minced
1 stalk celery, chopped
1 pound ground lamb
2 tablespoons chopped
 fresh herbs (parsley,
 basil, thyme, and
 rosemary)

Salt and pepper to taste
½ cup bread crumbs
¼ cup grated Parmesan
 cheese
¼ cup crumbled feta
 cheese
¼ cup shredded
 mozzarella
¼ cup pistachio nuts,
 chopped

Slice the eggplants in half and scoop out the pulp, leaving the very thin shells all in one piece. Place the eggplant flesh in a bowl, sprinkle generously with salt, and let sit 30 minutes. Parboil the shells and drain the eggplant flesh. Preheat oven to 375°F. Pour the olive oil into a heavy skillet and sauté the onion, garlic, celery, and ground lamb until the meat is browned. Add the chopped herbs and season with salt and pepper. Stir in the bread crumbs and Parmesan cheese. (If the mixture seems dry, moisten with a few tablespoons of lamb or beef stock.) Stir in the feta and mozzarella cheese and the pistachios. Spoon the mixture into the parboiled shells and place the shells in a shallow baking dish. Bake 20-30 minutes. *Serves 4.*

MIRROR LAKE INN
Lake Placid, New York

ROAST LEG OF SPRING LAMB

Vegetables added to the lamb as it cooks provide extra flavor to the pan juices. Use a rack or put the lamb directly in a roasting pan.

1 leg of lamb, preferably boned and rolled	Salt and pepper to taste
1 clove garlic	1 medium onion, peeled and sliced
Powdered mustard to taste	1 carrot, peeled and sliced

Preheat oven to 500°F. Rub the lamb with garlic and sprinkle with the mustard and salt and pepper to taste. Place in a roasting pan and add the onion and carrot slices. Sear the meat 10 minutes. Reduce oven temperature to 300°F. and roast the meat, uncovered, allowing 20 minutes per pound. (Use a meat thermometer to test doneness. At 140°F. the lamb is rare, at 150°F. medium, and at 160°F. well done.) Remove the lamb from the pan. Discard the vegetables. Make a gravy with the pan drippings according to your favorite recipe.   *Serves 10-12.*

BUTTERNUT INN
Chaffee, New York

TARRAGON-HERB LAMB CHOPS

A refreshing change from the standard herbs one expects with lamb. The amount of mustard seed left on the chops after cooking is up to the cook's discretion; it's easy to rub off, and doing so will enhance the appearance and texture of the final dish.

¼ cup olive oil
¼ cup tarragon vinegar
3 tablespoons mustard
  seed
3 tablespoons chopped
  fresh tarragon or
1 tablespoon dried

2 cloves garlic, crushed
Salt and pepper to taste
8 loin lamb chops
  (approximately
  6 ounces each)

In a glass or enamel bowl combine all the ingredients except the lamb chops. Arrange the chops in a shallow glass pan and pour the marinade over them. Marinate at least 8 hours, preferably overnight. Broil or grill to taste.

Serves 4.

SIDE DISHES

Winter Clove Inn, Round Top, New York

GENEVA ON THE LAKE
Geneva, New York

RICE MARRAKECH

An excellent accompaniment for grilled meats, lamb, curries, and seafood dishes. Toasted almonds and cashews will enhance the flavor; add them at the end of the sautéing step.

6 cups chicken stock	1 clove garlic, minced
1 cup cracked wheat bulgur	6 shallots, minced
1 cup (2 sticks) butter	½ cup finely chopped mint leaves
2 cups Uncle Ben's converted rice, uncooked	½ cup finely chopped fresh parsley
½ cup almonds	2 tablespoons ground cinnamon
½ cup cashews	1 tablespoon white pepper

Heat 1 cup of the stock to boiling. Add it to the bulgur and set aside. In a large, heavy kettle or Dutch oven with a tight-fitting lid melt the butter. Add the rice, nuts, garlic, and shallots and sauté, stirring frequently, over medium heat until golden, about 15 minutes. Add the remaining ingredients. Reduce heat and cook, covered, 20 minutes. Uncover and stir in the bulgur. Cover and let stand 10 minutes before serving. *Serves 12-14.*

MOHONK MOUNTAIN HOUSE
New Paltz, New York

MUSHROOM CURRY

Tasty and satisfying, an especially good dish to serve with a Middle Eastern dinner. The inn also makes this dish with 1½ cups raw bulgur wheat; increase baking time if you make this substitution.

½ pound mushrooms
3 tablespoons butter
1 onion, chopped
1 tablespoon curry powder
2 apples, cored and chopped

Paprika
2 cups cooked, hot rice
2⅔ cups yogurt or sour cream

Preheat oven to 350°F. Chop the mushroom stems and leave the caps whole. In a heavy skillet melt 2 tablespoons of the butter and sauté the mushroom caps for about 5 minutes. Set aside. Add the remaining 1 tablespoon of butter and sauté the onion and curry powder until the onion is soft. Add one of the chopped apples to the pan along with the mushroom stems and sprinkle with paprika. Cook over low heat for several minutes. Don't let the apple get mushy. Place the cooked rice in a greased 1½-quart baking dish. Spread the mushrooms, onion, cooked apple, and yogurt evenly on top. Bake 10-15 minutes or until the sauce is firm. Sprinkle remaining chopped apple on top before serving.   *Serves 6.*

GOLD MOUNTAIN CHALET
Spring Glen, New York

TOFU MUSHROOM STEW

An easy-to-make and very filling dish to serve with brown rice or another vegetable entrée.

3 tablespoons soy sauce	½ cup chopped onion
2 tablespoons peanut butter	½ cup chopped green pepper
1 teaspoon onion powder	½ cup chopped carrots
1 clove garlic, minced	½ cup chopped mushrooms
1 pound fresh, firm tofu, cubed	Mushroom Sauce (recipe follows)
¼ cup oil	
½ cup chopped celery	

In a small bowl combine the soy sauce, peanut butter, onion powder, and garlic. Coat the cubed tofu in the mixture. Pour the oil into a heavy skillet and brown the tofu. Add the celery, onion, green pepper, carrots, and mushrooms and continue cooking, stirring constantly, until the onion is soft. Serve topped with Mushroom Sauce. *Serves 4.*

MUSHROOM SAUCE

3 tablespoons butter	1 cup vegetable or potato peel broth
½ pound mushrooms, diced	½ cup half-and-half
5 tablespoons flour	

In a heavy saucepan or small skillet melt the butter. Sauté the mushrooms until tender. Sprinkle in the flour, coating the mushrooms. Stir until smooth. Add the broth and bring to a boil, stirring constantly. Remove from heat and add the half-and-half.

THE BAKERS
Stone Ridge, New York

COUNTRY POTATOES (LINDA'S STYLE)

Doug and Linda Baker do not peel the potatoes when preparing this recipe or the one that appears on the following page. To peel or not to peel is a decision the cook should make. If you do peel your potatoes ahead of time, keep them in cold water until cooking so they won't darken. Use leftover cooked potatoes in omelets, soups, yeast breads, to thicken stews, and to form mashed potato crusts for dishes containing gravy.

5 to 10 medium potatoes, baked
2 to 4 tablespoons butter
1 tablespoon garlic juice
Salt to taste

Slice the baked potatoes into wedges. In a heavy skillet melt the butter, add the garlic juice, and brown the potatoes evenly on all sides. Season with salt.   *Serves 6-8.*

THE BAKERS
Stone Ridge, New York

COUNTRY POTATOES (DOUG'S STYLE)

Bacon fat brings a fine flavor to these crispy, golden potato slices. Serve at any meal — with ham or Canadian bacon for breakfast or with broiled steak or chops for dinner. Chef Doug Baker uses lemon pepper for an interesting twist.

Bacon grease   Salt and pepper to taste
1½ to 2 pounds russet
  potatoes, washed and
  sliced ¼ inch thick

Preheat oven to 400°F. Brush a large baking sheet or shallow roasting pan with bacon grease. Arrange a single layer of potatoes on the greased sheet or in the pan. Brush the tops of the potatoes with additional bacon grease and season lightly with salt and pepper. Bake 10-15 minutes until golden brown. Flip slices over, brush again with bacon grease, and bake until brown.   *Serves 3-4.*

THE OLD DUTCH INN
Kinderhook, New York

GRATIN DAUPHINOISE

This creamy casserole of potatoes layered with cheese makes an elegant addition to any meal. It reheats very well.

1 quart (4 cups) heavy
   cream
1 quart milk
9 large russet potatoes,
   peeled and sliced
4 to 5 cloves garlic,
   chopped

1 ½ tablespoons salt
¼ teaspoon white pepper
⅛ teaspoon grated
   nutmeg
3 cups grated or sliced
   Gruyère or Swiss cheese

In a large, heavy saucepan or pot combine the cream, milk, and potatoes. Add the garlic, salt, pepper, and nutmeg. Bring to a boil, reduce heat, and simmer, stirring occasionally, until the potatoes are tender. Preheat oven to 325°F. Transfer the potatoes and sauce to a baking dish, layering them alternately with the cheese. Finish with a layer of cheese on top. Bake until golden brown, approximately 30 minutes.   *Serves 8-10.*

MIRROR LAKE INN
Lake Placid, New York

ANNA POTATOES

A fine side dish, nicely seasoned and colored by the paprika. The results do not give away how easy this dish is to prepare. The hardest thing about it is slicing the potatoes! If you have a machine to help, make a large quantity.

2 pounds (6 medium) potatoes, peeled and thinly sliced	2 tablespoons butter, melted
½ cup chicken broth	Grated Parmesan cheese
Salt and pepper to taste	Paprika

Preheat oven to 350°F. Line a 9-inch round casserole with sliced potatoes. Add the chicken broth and season with salt and pepper. Brush the top with melted butter and sprinkle with Parmesan cheese and paprika. Cover tightly and bake 1 hour. Remove the cover and broil until brown.   *Serves 6-8.*

HUDSON HOUSE
Cold Spring, New York

SAFFRON MUSHROOM POTATOES

Carving as well as cooking skills come into play with this most unusual way to fix potatoes. Save the trimmings for home fries.

10 red potatoes	6 black peppercorns
Pinch of saffron	1 quart water or chicken
1 bay leaf	stock
1 tablespoon thyme	Salt to taste

Wash the potatoes. Insert an apple corer halfway into the potato (lengthwise), and turn once. With a paring knife carefully cut into the center of the potato (width-wise) until its blade hits the apple corer. Then turn the knife all the way around and remove excess potato. The idea here is to cut the potato to resemble a mushroom. In a large kettle or saucepan simmer the potatoes in the remaining ingredients 20 minutes or until tender. Do not overcook, or the stems will fall off the "mushrooms."

Serves 6-8.

THE 1770 HOUSE
East Hampton, New York

CARROT FRITTERS

Similar to potato pancakes, loaded with the flavor of fresh carrots. Other vegetables such as summer squash or zucchini can be substituted for the carrots; shred, salt, and squeeze out excess moisture from the squash before proceeding.

5 to 6 small to medium carrots, grated	1 tablespoon sugar
	¼ cup flour
2 eggs	¼ cup sweet butter
½ teaspoon salt	

In a medium bowl combine the grated carrots, eggs, salt, and sugar. Beat until well mixed. Blend in the flour and stir. In a large skillet melt the butter until hot and drop in the batter by tablespoons. Fry the fritters for a few minutes on each side. Remove with a slotted spoon, place on a platter lined with paper towels, and keep warm in the oven until all the fritters are cooked.   *Serves 4.*

THE MERRILL MAGEE HOUSE
Warrensburg, New York

SUMMER SQUASH CASSEROLE

Squash holds up well in this dish and does not become too soft. Other vegetables such as zucchini, cauliflower, carrots, and broccoli can be substituted for the squash.

2 cups firm, coarsely
   chopped, cooked yellow
   squash
6 tablespoons butter
2 eggs
1 teaspoon salt
1 medium onion, chopped

1 cup shredded Swiss
   cheese
½ teaspoon nutmeg
1 cup evaporated milk
2 cups coarse, fresh bread
   crumbs
Butter

Preheat oven to 375°F. In a large bowl combine the squash, 6 tablespoons butter, eggs, salt, onion, shredded cheese, nutmeg, milk, and 1 cup of the bread crumbs. Mix well. Pour the mixture into a greased 1½-quart casserole. Sprinkle the remaining 1 cup bread crumbs over the top. Dot with butter and bake 30-40 minutes. *Serves 6-8.*

DEPUY CANAL HOUSE
High Falls, New York

BEER-BATTERED PUMPKIN WITH MAPLE SYRUP

Pumpkin is a far more versatile food than many people realize. Here's a novel way to serve it that's especially good with ham. Be sure not to overcook the pumpkin, or it won't hold up during frying.

1 pumpkin (6 pounds), top cut open and seeds removed	Oil for frying
	Powdered sugar
	Cottage cheese
Beer Batter (recipe follows)	Maple syrup

Preheat oven to 400°F. Place the pumpkin on a baking sheet or in a shallow baking dish and bake 1 hour or until tender to the touch but not mushy. While the pumpkin bakes, prepare the Beer Batter. Remove the pumpkin from the oven and cool in the refrigerator. When thoroughly cool, cut the pumpkin into triangles, leaving the skin intact. (A 6-pound pumpkin should make at least 10 triangles.)

Pour the oil into a deep-fat fryer and heat to 300°F. Have on hand the Beer Batter, powdered sugar in a flat dish, cottage cheese, and maple syrup. Dip the pumpkin pieces into the powdered sugar, then into the Beer Batter. Deep fry the pieces until golden brown. Put a scoop of cottage cheese on top of each triangle and make a small well in the cottage cheese. Fill the well with maple syrup and serve.   *Serves 10-12.*

BEER BATTER

1 cup flour	½ teaspoon nutmeg
1 teaspoon salt	1 can (12 ounces) beer

In a medium bowl sift the flour, salt, and nutmeg into the beer. Mix until the batter is frothy. Allow to stand at least 1 hour (2 or 3 hours is recommended). Stir again before using.

MOHONK MOUNTAIN HOUSE
New Paltz, New York

MOHONK RELISH

A good way to use up an abundant cabbage harvest. Season to taste with salt, sugar, and vinegar.

1 large head cabbage, shredded	1 tablespoon white mustard seed
6 green peppers, cored and chopped	Salt
1 red pepper, cored and chopped	Sugar Vinegar

In a large glass or nonmetallic bowl combine the cabbage and peppers. Sprinkle with the mustard seed and salt and sugar to taste. Toss until well mixed. Slowly add vinegar to taste and mix again. Let sit for several hours before serving. *Makes 6 cups.*

UNION HALL INN
Johnstown, New York

MARINATED BAKED EGGPLANT

Serve as a vegetable dish or as an appetizer.

4 garlic cloves, mashed
½ cup oil
2 eggplants (about 2½ to
  3 pounds total), cubed
3 large, ripe tomatoes,
  thinly sliced

Salt and pepper to taste
2 teaspoons minced fresh
  rosemary
Vinegar and Oil Dressing
  (recipe follows)

Preheat oven to 250°F. Mix the garlic with the oil. Pour over the eggplant, toss well, and arrange in a 5x7-inch baking dish along with the sliced tomatoes. Sprinkle with the salt and pepper to taste and the rosemary. Bake 20 minutes. Remove from oven. Pour the Vinegar and Oil Dressing over the warm eggplant. Season with salt and pepper if desired. Marinate 1 hour before serving.

Serves 8-10.

VINEGAR AND OIL DRESSING

½ cup wine vinegar
½ cup oil
1 heaping tablespoon
  grated onion

Pinch of crushed red
  pepper

Combine all the ingredients in a jar with a tight-fitting lid. Shake until smooth.

WINTER CLOVE INN
Round Top, New York

CORN PUDDING

A lovely, custardlike dish and a fine way to use leftover corn. You can make this recipe with canned or frozen corn, but for the real thing use only corn off the cob. If you make this dish ahead of time, refrigerate it about 2 hours and bring it up to room temperature before baking.

3 eggs	½ teaspoon salt
3 cups fresh corn, cut from the cob	½ teaspoon freshly ground pepper
2 cups heavy cream	Paprika
1 teaspoon sugar	

Preheat oven to 350°F. In a large bowl beat the eggs slightly. Add the corn, cream, sugar, salt, and pepper and mix well. Pour the mixture into a buttered 2½-quart baking dish. Bake 1 hour or until a knife inserted in the center comes out clean. Sprinkle with paprika and serve.

Serves 6.

DEPUY CANAL HOUSE
High Falls, New York

DRIED TOMATO PUDDING

Chef John Novi developed this novel way of using dried tomatoes (and stretching them), which are priced beyond the budget for many home cooks. Prepare this dish in advance and keep it in the refrigerator as a special side dish or garnish. The dried tomato flavor goes well with veal, chicken, or pork.

1 quart dried tomatoes in olive oil	¼ cup warm water (approximately 110°F.)
¼ cup molasses	1 teaspoon baking soda
¼ cup flour	

Chop the tomatoes. In a double boiler or pan over simmering water combine all the ingredients and cook slowly for 6 hours, stirring occasionally. Cool. Pour into a container with a tight-fitting lid and store in the refrigerator until ready to use. *Makes 4 cups.*

THE 1770 HOUSE
East Hampton, New York

TOMATOES COUNTRY-STYLE

A crunchy crust covers a moist sandwich of tomatoes with a surprise center of cream cheese and herbs. Serve immediately as an appetizer or unusual side dish. If the tomatoes sit, the breading becomes soggy. The inn has made this recipe one of its regular dishes; this version is based on the first recipe ever published in Better Homes and Gardens. *Its creator received $3 as a prize.*

1 clove garlic, minced	½ cup flour
¼ cup minced fresh parsley	1 egg, beaten with ½ cup milk
⅛ teaspoon salt	⅔ cup dry bread crumbs
1 package (8 ounces) cream cheese, softened	3 tablespoons butter
1 teaspoon chopped fresh or dried basil	3 tablespoons olive oil
4 large tomatoes	Fresh basil or parsley for garnish (optional)

In a food processor or with a mixer beat together the garlic, parsley, salt, cream cheese, and basil. Slice the tomatoes into 10 even slices, each about ¼ inch thick. Spread 5 slices with about 2 tablespoons of the cream cheese mixture each. Top with the remaining 5 tomato slices to make 5 sandwiches. Dip each sandwich into the flour, then into the beaten egg, and finally into the crumbs, coating each side with each ingredient. In a heavy skillet combine the butter and oil and fry the tomato sandwiches on both sides over medium heat until brown. Garnish with fresh basil or parsley if desired.

Serves 4-5.

NEW YORK STATE INNS

DEPUY CANAL HOUSE
High Falls, New York

PASTA WITH DAY LILY PESTO

Chef John Novi is known for using surprising ingredients in the kitchen, and he doesn't let anyone down with this recipe. He shares this information about day lilies: Both wild and domestic day lilies grow in abundance throughout New York and the rest of the Northeast. They appear along the roadside in late March or early April and can be identified by their very bright green color. When they are 2 to 3 inches tall, their leaves begin to open out, and they assume a crown-like appearance. Gather day lily shoots from late March through May and use them in any dish calling for asparagus. The shoots are especially tasty when no more than 1 to 6 inches tall. Cut them at ground level with a sharp knife; this does not injure the plant, which will continue to produce shoots from its bulb. Almost every part of the day lily is edible, including the buds and flowers, which are delightful in soups or when dipped in tempura batter and fried.

1 pound pasta (linguini or
   thin spaghetti)
1 cup heavy cream
1 cup Day Lily Pesto
   (recipe follows)

4 tablespoons pecorino
   cheese (or more to taste)

242 / Side Dishes

In a large pot boil the pasta according to the package directions. As the pasta cooks, heat a sauté pan over medium heat. Add the cream and boil 4-6 minutes until thickened and reduced to about ¾ cup. Add the pesto and stir until hot. Drain the pasta and pour into a large bowl. Add half the pesto and cream mixture and half the cheese to the pasta. Toss until well mixed. Put the pasta into 4 heated bowls and top with the remaining pesto and cheese. Serve immediately. *Serves 4.*

DAY LILY PESTO

This recipe makes more than you'll need for the above dish. Store leftover pesto in a closed container in the refrigerator.

½ pound day lily sprouts (or the bottom 6 inches of more mature plants)
¼ pound fresh spinach, washed, stems removed, and dried
1 cup olive oil

3 cloves garlic
½ cup pine nuts or walnuts (toasted if desired)
6 tablespoons pecorino cheese
1 cup heavy cream

In a blender or food processor purée the day lily sprouts, spinach leaves, and oil. Add the garlic, nuts, cheese, and cream and blend until smooth.

Makes 2½ cups.

DESSERTS

The Redcoat's Return, Elka Park, New York

PIES

HUDSON HOUSE
Cold Spring, New York

DOUBLE FUDGE PIE

A very rich chocolate pie, best served warm, topped with vanilla ice cream.

1 cup sugar
3 large eggs
½ cup light corn syrup
½ cup heavy cream or
  whipping cream
½ cup unsweetened cocoa
  powder

3 tablespoons unsalted
  butter, melted
1 teaspoon vanilla
¼ teaspoon salt
9-inch pie shell, unbaked
½ cup semisweet
  chocolate pieces

Preheat oven to 350°F. In a large bowl combine the sugar, eggs, corn syrup, cream, cocoa, butter, vanilla, and salt. Mix well. Pour the mixture into the unbaked pie shell. Scatter the chocolate pieces over the top. Bake 40-45 minutes or until a knife inserted in the center comes out clean. *Makes one 9-inch pie.*

KITTLE HOUSE
Mount Kisco, New York

WHITE CHOCOLATE MOUSSE PIE

A divinely light and creamy pie. Dress it up with semi-sweet chocolate shavings or cutouts.

CRUST

1 cup graham cracker
crumbs
¼ pound white chocolate

2 to 2½ tablespoons
butter, melted

Preheat oven to 350°F. Mix the crumbs with the chocolate and butter until moist enough to press into a greased 10-inch pie pan. Bake 5-10 minutes or until lightly browned. Be careful not to burn the crust.

FILLING

½ pound white chocolate
¼ cup water
2 egg yolks
1½ tablespoons white
crème de cacao

¼ cup sugar
1 cup heavy cream

Over hot water in the top of a double boiler combine the white chocolate and water. Heat until the chocolate melts. In a heavy saucepan over low heat cook the egg yolks, crème de cacao, and sugar until thick. Combine the melted chocolate and the egg mixture and stir until smooth. Set aside to cool. Whip the cream and fold into the chocolate mixture. Turn the filling into the pie shell and chill at least 4 hours before serving.

Makes one 10-inch pie.

ROUNDUP RANCH
Downsville, New York

PEANUT BUTTER PIE

Two layers of peanut butter separated by a smooth, creamy pudding. For a special treat, use extra-crunchy peanut butter.

⅔ cup confectioners' sugar	1 tablespoon cornstarch
⅓ cup crunchy peanut butter	2 egg yolks, beaten
9-inch pie shell, baked	2 cups milk
⅓ cup granulated sugar	1 tablespoon butter
1 tablespoon flour	1 teaspoon vanilla
	Whipped cream for topping

In a medium bowl combine the confectioners' sugar and peanut butter and mix together until crumbly. Sprinkle half the crumbs in the bottom of the baked pie shell. In a medium saucepan combine the granulated sugar, flour, and cornstarch. Add the beaten egg yolks and mix over low heat to form a smooth paste. Add the milk and cook, stirring constantly, until thickened. Remove from the heat and stir in the butter and vanilla. Pour the filling on top of the crumb mixture in the baked pie shell. Cool thoroughly. Sprinkle the top of the filling with the remaining peanut butter crumbs. Serve with whipped cream. *Makes one 9-inch pie.*

MIRROR LAKE INN
Lake Placid, New York

BETTY'S PEANUT BUTTER PIE

The inn features this recipe, which came from an owner of the Oyster Steamer restaurant in Anna Maria, Florida. At Mirror Lake they make a number of pies at once, using Cool Whip and pie shells made from chocolate cookie crumbs. We've reduced their recipe and substituted whipped cream.

1 package (3 ounces)
cream cheese, softened
¾ cup confectioners'
sugar
⅔ cup creamy peanut
butter
⅓ cup milk

1½ cups heavy cream,
whipped
9-inch pie shell, baked
Whipped cream and
chopped or whole
peanuts for garnish

Cream together the cream cheese and sugar. Add the peanut butter, milk, and whipped cream. Blend well and pour into the baked pie shell. Chill 4 hours. Just before serving top with additional whipped cream and chopped or whole peanuts.   *Makes one 9-inch pie.*

THE MANDANA INN
Skaneateles, New York

PEANUT BUTTER CREAM CHEESE PIE

The Mandana Inn introduced this recipe during the Carter administration. It proved to be so popular that the chef kept it as a permanent addition to the menu. The sweetness and intensity of the peanut butter flavor will vary according to the brand of peanut butter used. You can increase the amount of peanut butter slightly without affecting the final result. For variation, serve in individual milk chocolate shells and pipe the mixture in with a star tip.

½ cup peanut butter
½ cup cream cheese
3 tablespoons superfine
 sugar
1 tablespoon vanilla
1 pint (2 cups) heavy
 cream, whipped

9-inch graham cracker
 crust
Chopped peanuts for
 garnish

In a medium bowl combine the peanut butter, cream cheese, sugar, and vanilla. Mix well to form a smooth batter. Fold in the whipped cream. (To make this job easier, you can beat half the whipped cream into the peanut butter mixture to lighten it and then fold in the rest of the whipped cream.) Pour the mixture into the crust and sprinkle with chopped peanuts. Chill well before serving. *Makes one 9-inch pie.*

PEANUT BUTTER ICE CREAM PIE

A quick and easy recipe, which the inn says is its all-time best seller. For a special treat, top it with your own special fudge sauce.

1 quart French vanilla ice cream	¼ cup chopped, unsalted peanuts
½ cup chunky peanut butter	Hot fudge sauce
1 teaspoon vanilla	Whipped cream
Graham Cracker Crust (recipe follows)	

In a large bowl soften the ice cream until it can be stirred with a spoon. Fold in the peanut butter and vanilla until well mixed. Pour the mixture into the Graham Cracker Crust. Sprinkle with chopped nuts. Freeze until solid. Top individual servings with hot fudge sauce and whipped cream.   *Makes one 9-inch pie.*

GRAHAM CRACKER CRUST

1 ¾ cups fine graham cracker crumbs	½ teaspoon cinnamon
⅓ cup sugar	½ cup (1 stick) butter, melted

Combine all the ingredients. Press into a deep 9-inch cake pan.

THE REDCOAT'S RETURN
Elka Park, New York

COFFEE TOFFEE PIE

A delightful two-layer dessert for coffee lovers. This recipe also will work if you double the amount of filling and halve the amount of topping. The inn recommends making the pie in advance and chilling it overnight to firm up the filling, but you can get away with a 2-hour chilling time for both the topping and the filling.

CRUST

1 cup flour	¼ cup brown sugar
½ teaspoon salt	¾ cup ground walnuts
½ cup shortening	1 tablespoon ice water

Preheat oven to 375°F. In a medium bowl combine the flour and salt. Cut in the shortening until the mixture becomes crumbly. Stir in the brown sugar and walnuts, sprinkle with the ice water, and mix quickly. Pack the mixture into a greased 10-inch pie pan. Bake 15 minutes or until the crust is firm.

FILLING

½ cup (1 stick) butter	2 tablespoons loose
½ cup sugar	instant coffee
1 square unsweetened	2 eggs
chocolate, melted	

With an electric mixer beat the butter until creamy. Add the sugar and beat until fluffy. Blend in the melted chocolate and coffee. Add 1 egg and beat 5 minutes. Add the second egg and beat 5 minutes longer. Pour the filling into the baked pie shell, cover, and chill overnight.

TOPPING

2 cups heavy cream	½ cup confectioners'
2 tablespoons loose	sugar
instant coffee	1 tablespoon dark rum

In a mixing bowl combine all four ingredients and beat until smooth. Chill. Then beat until stiff. Swirl on top of the chilled filling and chill again for 2 hours. Serve very cold. *Makes one 10-inch pie.*

ASA RANSOM HOUSE
Clarence, New York

KAHLÚA CHIFFON PIE

Divinely light and satiny smooth, this is a fine dessert for a holiday or special occasion. The inn uses a chocolate crumb crust, but a baked pie shell also will work well.

¼ cup water
2 ½ teaspoons unflavored
  gelatin
⅓ cup Kahlúa
4 eggs, separated
⅔ cup sugar

¾ cup heavy cream
10-inch pie shell, baked
Whipped cream and
  shaved chocolate for
  garnish

In a small saucepan combine the water and gelatin. Stir and let sit several minutes until the gelatin softens. Add the Kahlúa. In a medium bowl beat the egg yolks with ⅓ cup of the sugar until thick. Add the egg and sugar to the mixture in the saucepan and cook over low heat until the gelatin dissolves. Cool. Beat the egg whites with the remaining ⅓ cup sugar until stiff peaks form. Set aside. Beat the heavy cream until stiff. In a large bowl fold the whipped cream, beaten whites, and cooled gelatin mixture together. Pour into a baked and cooled pie shell and chill until set. Cover each serving with whipped cream and shaved chocolate.   *Makes one 10-inch pie.*

THE OLD DUTCH INN
Kinderhook, New York

BERRY CHIFFON PIE

A good summer dessert, this fluffy cream pie is filled with an assortment of fruit. Don't cheat: The crème de cassis is an important ingredient to get the flavor just right.

3 pints heavy cream	2 cups chopped
2 packages (10 ounces	strawberries
each) frozen	2 cups blueberries
raspberries, thawed	2 nine-inch graham
1 teaspoon almond extract	cracker crusts, baked
1 tablespoon vanilla	and cooled
Crème de cassis	Fresh strawberries, sliced,
¼ cup superfine sugar	for garnish
1 package (8 ounces)	
vanilla instant pudding	

Whip the cream until soft peaks form. Drain the juice from the raspberries into a measuring cup. Add the almond extract, vanilla, and enough crème de cassis to make 1 cup of liquid. Blend this liquid and the sugar into the whipped cream. Fold the pudding into the cream mixture. Fold in the raspberries, strawberries, and blueberries. Spoon the mixture into the graham cracker crusts and chill well before serving. Garnish with slices of fresh strawberries. *Makes two 9-inch pies.*

GREENVILLE ARMS
Greenville, New York

LEMON SOUR CREAM PIE

A sweet and tangy dessert. If you really love lemon, increase the amount of lemon juice by several tablespoons.

1 cup sugar	1 cup milk
4 tablespoons cornstarch	3 egg yolks, slightly beaten
1 tablespoon grated lemon	1 cup sour cream
peel	9-inch pie shell, baked
¼ cup lemon juice (or	Whipped cream, lemon
more to taste)	slices, and mint sprigs
¼ cup butter, melted	for garnish

In a medium saucepan combine the sugar, cornstarch, lemon peel, lemon juice, butter, milk, and egg yolks. Cook, stirring constantly, until thick. Remove from heat. Cover the pan with plastic wrap or waxed paper to prevent a skin from forming on the mixture and cool thoroughly. Fold in the sour cream. Pour the mixture into a baked and cooled pie shell. Chill several hours. Serve topped with whipped cream, lemon slices, and mint sprigs. *Makes one 9-inch pie.*

OLD DROVERS INN
Dover Plains, New York

KEY LIME PIE

Olin Potter, creator of this inn in its twentieth-century incarnation, began wintering in the Florida Keys just after World War II. He brought this recipe back to New York with him. It uses commonly available limes rather than the authentic key limes, which are small and very tart. One of the essential ingredients is condensed milk; don't try it with fresh milk, or you'll have a mess on your hands. To add some color, garnish the pie with whipped cream and a sprinkling of grated lime peel.

5 egg yolks
19 ounces (about 1¼ cans) sweetened, condensed milk
½ cup freshly squeezed lime juice (from about 4 limes)

Grated peel of 1 lime
8-inch graham cracker crust

In a medium bowl beat the egg yolks with a wire whisk until foamy. Blend in the condensed milk, lime juice, and grated lime peel and stir to form a smooth mixture. Pour the mixture into the graham cracker crust and chill at least 2 hours before serving.   *Makes one 8-inch pie.*

BEAR MOUNTAIN INN
Bear Mountain, New York

DEEP-DISH APPLE PIE

For a pleasant change, make these individual servings for pie lovers. Vary the amount of sugar according to the sweetness of the apples. Larger ramekins can be used for heartier portions.

6 apples, peeled and sliced
2 tablespoons sugar
Dash of nutmeg
2 teaspoons cinnamon

¼ cup water
Egg Wash (recipe follows)
1 package frozen puff
   pastry, thawed

In a medium bowl combine the apples, sugar, nutmeg, cinnamon, and water. Let the mixture soak 4-6 hours, allowing the apples to become slightly limp. Preheat oven to 350°F. Spoon the mixture into eight 6-ounce custard cups or ramekins. Brush the Egg Wash around the rim of each cup. Top each cup with a 4x4-inch sheet of puff pastry. Brush the Egg Wash over the top of the pastry. Bake 15-20 minutes or until the dough is golden brown.

Serves 8.

EGG WASH

1 egg
2 tablespoons milk

Dash of salt

In a small bowl beat the egg and milk until foamy. Season with the salt.

WINTER CLOVE INN
Round Top, New York

INDIAN SUMMER PIE

Mincemeat provides a pleasant surprise on the bottom of this dessert, which combines several old-fashioned flavors. Serve with whipped cream or ice cream.

¼ pound cooking apples, cored and diced
½ pound mincemeat
3 tablespoons sherry
2 cups cooked and puréed or canned pumpkin
1 cup sugar
1 cup milk

2 eggs, slightly beaten
½ teaspoon salt
1 teaspoon cinnamon
1 teaspoon allspice
½ teaspoon ginger
1½ teaspoons butter, melted
9-inch pie shell, unbaked

Preheat oven to 350°F. In a medium bowl combine the apples, mincemeat, and sherry. Mix well. In a second bowl combine all the remaining ingredients. Mix thoroughly. Pour the mincemeat mixture into the unbaked pie shell. Pour the pumpkin mixture on top of the mincemeat. Bake 45 minutes or until firm. *Makes one 9-inch pie.*

DEPUY CANAL HOUSE
High Falls, New York

NOVI'S FIG FUDGE PIE

Use a food processor if possible to mince the figs for this recipe. If you're using dried figs, soak them overnight in the cognac after chopping; if you're using fresh figs, which the chef recommends, soak them 1 hour. Rice syrup is used as the sweetening agent. If your local health food store doesn't carry it, substitute 2 cups sugar and cut back the number of eggs in the recipe to 4.

1 pound fresh figs or ½ pound dried	6 eggs
⅓ cup cognac	¼ teaspoon salt
3 ounces semisweet chocolate	¼ teaspoon vanilla
1 cup (2 sticks) butter	2 eight-inch pie shells, unbaked
2 cups rice syrup	Whipped cream for garnish

Mince the figs and soak them in the cognac. Preheat oven to 350°F. In a small saucepan melt the chocolate and butter. Pour into a bowl. Add the rice syrup or sugar, eggs, salt, vanilla, and figs, along with the cognac in which they were soaked. Blend well. Pour the mixture into the unbaked pie shells and bake 35-45 minutes. Cool and chill. Serve with whipped cream.

Makes two 8-inch pies.

CAKES AND COOKIES

THE HULBERT HOUSE
Boonville, New York

EASY CHOCOLATE CAKE

There's nothing difficult about this traditional favorite, which can be dressed up with frosting or served plain.

1 teaspoon vanilla	1 ½ cups flour
1 cup sugar	1 teaspoon baking soda
5 tablespoons oil or	½ teaspoon salt
shortening, melted	3 tablespoons cocoa
1 cup cold water	1 tablespoon vinegar

Preheat oven to 375°F. In a mixing bowl combine all the ingredients and beat at slow speed until the batter is smooth. Pour into a greased and floured 8-inch square pan and bake 25-30 minutes.

Makes one 8-inch square cake.

GREENVILLE ARMS
Greenville, New York

BEST EVER
CHOCOLATE FUDGE LAYER CAKE

Fudgy, moist, and delectable — everything a chocolate cake should be. To keep the cake from sticking, grease the pans and line them with waxed paper or parchment paper; grease the liner and dust it lightly with flour.

3 squares unsweetened chocolate	2¼ cups firmly packed brown sugar
2¼ cups sifted cake flour	3 eggs
2 teaspoons baking soda	1½ teaspoons vanilla
½ teaspoon salt	1 cup sour cream
½ cup (1 stick) butter, softened	1 cup boiling water
	Frosting (recipe follows)

Preheat oven to 375°F. In a double boiler over hot water melt the chocolate. Cool. Sift together the flour, baking soda, and salt. Cream together the butter and brown sugar. Add the eggs, one at a time, beating well after each addition. Add the vanilla and cooled chocolate. Stir in the dry ingredients alternately with the sour cream. Beat well. Stir in the boiling water. Pour the batter into 2 greased and floured (or paper-lined, greased, and floured) 9-inch layer pans. Bake 25 minutes or until the cake is done. Cool on wire racks for 10 minutes before removing from the pans. Cool completely before frosting.   *Makes one 9-inch, 2-layer cake.*

FROSTING

Professional cake decorators like to "seal" a cake with a very thin layer of frosting (called a crumb layer) before covering it with a thicker layer. To have enough frosting for a crumb layer and to make piped borders, increase each ingredient by one-half.

4 one-ounce squares unsweetened chocolate	½ cup milk
½ cup (1 stick) butter	2 teaspoons vanilla
1 pound confectioners' sugar	

In a small saucepan combine the chocolate and butter and stir over low heat until melted. In a medium bowl combine the confectioners' sugar, milk, and vanilla and stir until smooth. Add the chocolate mixture. Set the bowl in a pan of ice water and beat until the mixture is thick enough to spread on the cooled cake.

BIG MOOSE INN
Eagle Bay, New York

DELICIOUS CHOCOLATE SHEET CAKE

A moist fudge cake, reminiscent of brownies. Jane Rider from Delaware, a friend of the inn, sent this recipe along to the innkeepers.

1 cup (2 sticks) butter	1 teaspoon baking soda
¼ cup cocoa	½ teaspoon salt
1 cup water	2 eggs
¼ teaspoon cinnamon	½ cup sour cream
2 cups sifted flour	Frosting (recipe follows)
2 cups sugar	

In a large saucepan combine the butter, cocoa, water, and cinnamon. Bring to a boil, remove from heat, and add the flour, sugar, baking soda, and salt. Beat in the eggs and sour cream. Pour the batter into a greased and floured 9x13-inch cake pan and bake 35-40 minutes. Let the cake cool 5-7 minutes before frosting.

Makes one 9x13-inch sheet cake.

FROSTING

½ cup (1 stick) butter	1 pound confectioners'
5 tablespoons milk	sugar
¼ cup cocoa	1 teaspoon vanilla

In a medium saucepan combine the butter, milk, and cocoa. Bring to a boil, remove from heat, and stir in the confectioners' sugar and vanilla. Mix well and spread on the cooled cake.

THE KREBS
Skaneateles, New York

MOIST CHOCOLATE CAKE

Dress up this cake with your favorite frosting or serve it plain in the style of this venerable restaurant. To make sour milk, put 1 ½ teaspoons lemon juice or distilled white vinegar in the bottom of a glass measuring cup. Add enough milk to make ½ cup and let stand until the milk curdles.

½ cup cocoa
1 ½ cups cake flour
¼ teaspoon salt
1 cup sugar
1 teaspoon baking soda
½ cup (1 stick) butter, melted

1 teaspoon vanilla
1 egg
½ cup sour milk
½ cup hot water

Preheat oven to 350°F. In a medium bowl sift together the cocoa, flour, salt, sugar, and baking soda. Add the butter, vanilla, egg, sour milk, and hot water and stir several minutes. Pour batter into a greased and floured 8-inch square pan. Bake 35-40 minutes.

Makes one 8-inch square cake.

PARTRIDGE BERRY INN
Watertown, New York

CHEESECAKE

Smooth and satiny, a perfect dessert for a special occasion. The inn bakes its cheesecake in rectangular pans and serves slices topped with fruit sauce.

2 packages (16 ounces each) cream cheese, softened
1 cup sugar
4 eggs
1½ teaspoons vanilla

1½ teaspoons grated lemon peel
Crumb Crust (recipe follows)
Sour Cream Topping (recipe follows)

Preheat oven to 350°F. In a mixing bowl combine the softened cream cheese, sugar, and eggs and beat until frothy. Add the vanilla and lemon peel and beat well. Pour the mixture over the Crumb Crust. Bake 20-25 minutes or until a knife inserted in the center comes out clean. Cool. Cover with topping. Chill.

Makes one 9-inch cake.

CRUMB CRUST

1 cup graham cracker   ½ cup sugar
  crumbs
½ cup (1 stick) butter,
  melted

In a medium bowl combine all the ingredients and mix well. Press firmly into a 9-inch springform or round pan.

SOUR CREAM TOPPING

2 cups sour cream   1 tablespoon vanilla
½ cup sugar

In a medium bowl combine all the ingredients. Spread over the cooled cake with a rubber spatula.

THE POINT
Saranac Lake, New York

CHOCOLATE CHEESECAKE WITH CRÈME ANGLAISE

A nice change from standard cheesecakes, this one is very light and is made without a crust. Make as directed below or bake individual servings in 6-ounce ramekins. Be sure to let the cake sit after baking to give it time to solidify. Use only large eggs and make sure the cream cheese does not contain vegetable gum, which can affect the consistency.

2½ pounds cream cheese
1½ cups sugar
4 large eggs
1 teaspoon vanilla
6 ounces semisweet
   chocolate, melted

4 ounces unsweetened
   chocolate, melted
Softened butter and sugar
   to prepare baking dish
Crème Anglaise (recipe
   follows)

Preheat oven to 325°F. In a mixing bowl combine the cream cheese and sugar and whip until smooth. Scrape the bottom of the bowl to make sure there are no lumps. Add the eggs, one at a time, again scraping the bottom of the bowl to make sure the eggs are well blended into the mixture. Whip until smooth. Add the vanilla and melted chocolate and mix well. Butter a 2-quart round baking dish and sprinkle it with sugar. Pour the mixture into the dish and gently tap out the air. Place the baking dish in a pan of hot water and bake 2 hours. Let rest 30 minutes. Invert onto a serving platter. Serve individual slices on a pool of Crème Anglaise.   *Serves 8.*

CRÈME ANGLAISE

8 egg yolks	1 teaspoon vanilla
¾ cup sugar	3 tablespoons peppermint
1 cup milk, warmed	schnapps

In a medium bowl combine the egg yolks and sugar until smooth. Add the warm milk and mix. Whisk the mixture over a double boiler or pan of hot water until light in color and smooth. Cool. Add the vanilla and peppermint schnapps.

BUTTERNUT INN
Chaffee, New York

WHITE CHOCOLATE CHEESECAKE

The only sweetener in the filling for this recipe comes from the chocolate. If you've got a well-developed sweet tooth, add up to 1 cup sifted confectioners' sugar to make the cheesecake sweet but not cloying.

12 ounces white chocolate
½ cup milk
1 envelope unflavored
  gelatin
2 packages (8 ounces
  each) cream cheese
½ cup sour cream

½ teaspoon almond
  extract
½ cup heavy cream,
  whipped
Vanilla Crust (recipe
  follows)

In a heavy saucepan melt the chocolate. Set aside. Pour the milk into the pan, sprinkle with the gelatin, and let stand 1 minute. Then cook over low heat until the gelatin is dissolved. Set aside to cool. In a large mixing bowl combine the cream cheese, sour cream, and melted chocolate. Beat until very fluffy. Beat in the gelatin mixture and almond extract. Fold in the whipped cream. Pour into a crust-lined springform pan and chill at least 4 hours.   *Makes one 9-inch cake.*

VANILLA CRUST

2 cups finely crushed
  vanilla wafers
1 cup ground almonds

½ cup sugar
½ cup (1 stick) butter,
  melted

In a medium bowl combine all the ingredients. Form a lining for the cheesecake by pressing the mixture into a 9-inch springform pan, covering the bottom and coming 2 inches up the sides.

THE HEDGES
Blue Mountain Lake, New York

BUTTER CREAM FROSTING

Use as a filling between the layers of a chocolate cake, and you'll create a homemade Devil Dog. This frosting must be refrigerated.

½ cup (1 stick) butter
½ cup shortening
1 cup very fine sugar

2 eggs
1 teaspoon vanilla

In a mixing bowl combine all the ingredients. Beat 10 minutes or until the mixture is light and fluffy.

Makes 2½ cups.

SPRINGSIDE INN
Auburn, New York

SPRINGSIDE CHEESECAKE
WITH CHERRY TOPPING

This cake will keep well in the refrigerator for several days after it is baked. Add the sauce only when you're ready to serve it.

2 packages (8 ounces each) cream cheese, softened
2 eggs
¾ cup sugar

1 teaspoon vanilla
9-inch graham cracker crust
Fruit Topping (recipe follows)

Preheat oven to 350°F. In a mixing bowl combine the cream cheese, eggs, sugar, and vanilla. Mix 10 minutes at slow speed. Pour into the graham cracker crust. Place the baking pan in a larger container one-quarter full of hot water and bake 20-25 minutes. Cool. Serve with a spoonful of topping. *Makes one 9-inch cake.*

FRUIT TOPPING

1 can sour pitted cherries (or other fresh fruit)
1 cup sugar
3 tablespoons cornstarch

Drain the cherries and reserve a few tablespoons of juice. In a saucepan combine the drained cherries, sugar, and cornstarch. Add juice to thin as necessary. Bring to a boil and cook until the mixture reaches the desired consistency. Cool before spooning onto the cheesecake.

COUNTRY ROAD LODGE
Warrensburg, New York

HERBERT HOEGER'S APPLE RAISIN CAKE

This well-textured cake gets moister as it sits and can be kept for several days.

1½ cups oil	1 teaspoon salt
2 cups sugar	3 medium apples (cored
3 eggs	but unpeeled), thickly
1 teaspoon vanilla	sliced
3 cups unbleached flour	1 cup raisins
1 teaspoon baking soda	1 cup chopped walnuts
1 teaspoon cinnamon (or	Whipped cream
more to taste)	

Preheat oven to 350°F. In a mixing bowl combine the oil, sugar, eggs, and vanilla. Mix well. In a separate bowl combine the flour, baking soda, cinnamon, and salt to form a very stiff batter. Mix the dry ingredients into the wet. Stir the apples, raisins, and walnuts into the batter and spoon into a well-greased and floured Bundt pan. Bake 1-1¼ hours. Cool before removing from the pan. Serve plain or top with whipped cream.

Makes 1 Bundt cake.

THE HEDGES
Blue Mountain Lake, New York

GERMAN APPLE CAKE

Somewhat akin to a streusel, with better flavor (and easier to make!) than an apple pie. A perfect blend of apples and cinnamon, topped with a rich, buttery crust. Serve slightly warm, with vanilla ice cream.

1 ½ cups sifted flour	5 medium apples, peeled
1 cup sugar	and thinly sliced
Pinch of salt	¾ teaspoon cinnamon
½ cup (1 stick) butter	

Preheat oven to 425°F. In a medium bowl combine the flour, ½ cup of the sugar, salt, and butter and mix until crumbly. Measure out ¾ cup of the crumbs and set aside. Press the remaining crumbs into a 9-inch springform pan, covering the bottom and extending ¾ inch up the sides. In the bowl combine the apples, remaining ½ cup sugar, and cinnamon. Arrange in the shell. Bake 20 minutes. Remove from the oven, sprinkle the top with the ¾ cup crumbs, and bake 20 minutes longer or until lightly browned. *Makes one 9-inch cake.*

HUFF HOUSE
Roscoe, New York

APPLE CHIP CAKE

A moist cake that stays that way — delicious and crunchy. To dress it up, serve warm topped with whipped cream spiced with cinnamon. For extra richness, add 1 heaping tablespoon sour cream to the batter.

1½ cups oil	3 cups sifted flour
2 cups sugar	1 teaspoon vanilla
2 eggs	1 cup chopped nuts
½ teaspoon salt	3 cups peeled, chopped
1 teaspoon cinnamon	apples
1 teaspoon baking soda	

Preheat oven to 350°F. In a mixing bowl combine the oil, sugar, and eggs. Beat until smooth. Sift together the salt, cinnamon, baking soda, and flour and beat into the wet ingredients to form a stiff batter. Add the vanilla, chopped nuts, and chopped apples and stir to blend. Spoon the batter into a greased and floured 9x13-inch pan and bake 1 hour.   *Makes one 9x13-inch cake.*

BAYBERRY INN
Southampton, New York

CARROT CAKE

Moist and full-flavored, this traditional favorite is enhanced by the frosting. Use it to cover just the top or place the cake on a pedestal dish and frost the sides, too.

2 cups flour	3 eggs
2 teaspoons cinnamon	2 cups shredded carrots
2 teaspoons baking soda	1 small can crushed
½ teaspoon salt	pineapple, drained
¾ cup oil	½ cup coconut
2 cups sugar	Cream Cheese Frosting
1 cup lemon yogurt	(recipe follows)

Preheat oven to 350°F. In a medium bowl sift together the flour, cinnamon, baking soda, and salt. In a mixing bowl combine the oil, sugar, yogurt, and eggs and beat until smooth. Add the shredded carrots, drained pineapple, and coconut. Combine the dry ingredients with the wet and beat until smooth. Pour the mixture into a greased 10-inch tube pan and bake 1 hour. Cool and frost. *Makes one 10-inch cake.*

CREAM CHEESE FROSTING

1 package (3 ounces)	2 tablespoons heavy
cream cheese	cream
¼ cup butter, softened	
2 cups confectioners'	
sugar	

In a mixing bowl combine all the ingredients and beat until smooth, adding a bit more cream to the mixture if necessary to reach a spreading consistency.

Makes 1 ½ cups.

ROUNDUP RANCH
Downsville, New York

WACKY SNACK CAKE

A good cake to bake for a crowd. Serve cool or warm, with whipped cream or ice cream. This is a moist dessert that will keep well for several days. Cut the recipe in half to make one 9x13-inch cake, or quarter it for one 9x9-inch cake.

9 cups flour	2 tablespoons vinegar
6 cups sugar	2 tablespoons vanilla
3 cups cocoa	2 cups oil
2 tablespoons baking soda	6 cups cold water

Preheat oven to 350°F. In a large bowl combine the flour, sugar, cocoa, and baking soda. Beat in the vinegar, vanilla, oil, and cold water to form a smooth batter. Pour into a lightly greased 18x28-inch baking pan. Bake 30 minutes.   *Makes one 18x28-inch cake.*

THE 1770 HOUSE
East Hampton, New York

ZUCCOTTO CAKE

A dramatic dessert, especially when served with a spoon-ful of strawberries on the side. The filling is positively heav-enly. To simplify this recipe, use lady fingers as a substitute for the cake.

6 eggs	½ cup clarified butter
1 cup sugar	1 teaspoon vanilla
½ cup flour	Grand Marnier or brandy
½ cup cocoa	Filling (recipe follows)

Preheat oven to 375°F. Place the eggs and sugar in a mixing bowl and place the bowl over simmering water, stirring occasionally, until the eggs are warm and translucent. Attach the bowl to the mixer and beat on high 5 minutes or until tripled in volume. Reduce the speed, combine the flour and cocoa, and slowly add to the egg mixture. Fold in the butter and vanilla. Pour the mixture into a paper-lined jellyroll pan and bake 15-20 minutes.

Cut a 9-inch circle from the cooked cake and split it horizontally from the remaining cake. Cut 2 strips approximately 3 by 12 inches, and split them horizontally.

Place half of the 9-inch circle at the bottom of a 9-inch mixing bowl that has been lined with plastic wrap. Line the bowl completely with the four strips, arranging them lengthwise around the sides. Sprinkle the cake with Grand Marnier or brandy. Pour in the filling and smooth the top. Cover the top with the remaining circle of cake. Wrap tightly in plastic wrap and chill.   *Serves 12.*

FILLING

2 envelopes unflavored
  gelatin
¼ cup cold water
¼ cup Grand Marnier
1 cup half-and-half
3 egg yolks
½ cup sugar
⅓ cup flour
2 tablespoons butter

2 teaspoons vanilla
1 quart heavy cream
1½ cups sliced
  strawberries
4 squares semisweet
  chocolate, chopped
½ pound almond nougat
  or torrone, chopped
  (optional)

Dissolve the gelatin in the water and Grand Marnier. In a bowl over simmering water combine the half-and-half, egg yolks, sugar, and flour. Mix until thickened. Add the dissolved gelatin, butter, and vanilla. Whip the heavy cream and add the yolk mixture, blending until smooth. Add the strawberries, chocolate, and chopped nougat. Stir until evenly blended.

GARNET HILL
North River, New York

RASPBERRY TORTE

A rich, sweet dessert reminiscent of a Linzer Torte. The arrangement of the cake layers and filling requires some dexterity. To simplify the dessert but not spare the flavor, bake the cake as one 2-inch-thick layer in an 8-inch cake pan for 40 minutes at 350°F.; then top with preserves and cream.

1 cup graham cracker
  crumbs
½ cup chopped, moist
  coconut
½ cup chopped walnuts
4 egg whites
Pinch of salt
1 teaspoon vanilla
1 cup sugar

1 cup raspberry preserves
1 pint (2 cups) heavy
  cream, whipped with 1
  teaspoon unflavored
  gelatin softened in 1
  tablespoon water, or 1
  container (3½ cups)
  whipped topping

Preheat oven to 350°F. In a medium bowl combine the graham cracker crumbs, coconut, and walnuts and set aside. In a mixing bowl beat the egg whites with the salt and vanilla until foamy. Gradually add the sugar and continue beating until stiff peaks form. Fold the crumb mixture into the egg-white mixture. Spread the batter evenly into 3 well-greased 8-inch cake pans (or line the pans with greased parchment paper to eliminate any possibility of sticking). Bake approximately 30 minutes. Let cool. Remove the cake from the pans. Spread ⅓ of the preserves and whipped cream or topping on one layer. Put a second layer on top, spread with ⅓ of the preserves and whipped cream, and add the final layer. Cover the top with the remaining preserves and whipped cream. Refrigerate until ready to serve.

Makes one 8-inch, 3-layer cake.

GENESEE COUNTRY INN
Mumford, New York

SEVEN-UP CAKE

A rich, buttery pound cake with a mild lemon flavor, a favorite at the inn for conference luncheons. To add an extra touch, sprinkle it with powdered sugar or top with a lemon glaze.

1½ cups (3 sticks) butter	2 tablespoons lemon
3 cups sugar	extract
5 eggs	¾ cup Seven-Up
3 cups flour	

Preheat oven to 325°F. In a mixing bowl combine the butter and sugar and cream together until very smooth. Beat in the eggs, one at a time, and gradually mix in the flour and lemon extract. Fold in the Seven-Up. Pour the batter into a well-greased 12-cup Bundt pan. Bake 1-1¼ hours. Remove from the pan and cool before serving.

Serves 18-20.

THE ATHENAEUM
Chautauqua, New York

OATMEAL CAKE

Moist and tasty, fine to serve with coffee.

1 ⅞ cups boiling water
1 ½ cups rolled oats
½ cup (1 stick) butter
1 ½ cups granulated sugar
1 ½ cups brown sugar
1 ½ teaspoons vanilla
3 eggs

2 ¼ cups flour
1 ½ teaspoons baking soda
½ teaspoon salt
1 teaspoon cinnamon
1 teaspoon nutmeg
Lazy Dazy Frosting (recipe follows)

Combine the water and rolled oats and let sit 20 minutes. Preheat oven to 350°F. Cream together the butter and sugars until smooth. Add the vanilla and eggs and mix well. Add the softened oats. Sift together the flour, baking soda, salt, cinnamon, and nutmeg and add to the wet ingredients. Mix well. Pour the batter into a greased and floured 9-inch square pan and bake 50-55 minutes. While still warm frost with Lazy Dazy Frosting. Place under broiler until frosting is golden brown and bubbly.
Makes one 9-inch cake.

LAZY DAZY FROSTING

¼ cup butter, melted
½ cup brown sugar
3 tablespoons half-and-half

⅓ cup chopped nuts
¾ cup coconut

In a small bowl combine all the ingredients and mix until smooth. Spread on the warm cake.

THE HEDGES
Blue Mountain Lake, New York

OATMEAL COOKIES

These crisp, fragile cookies are best served with a mousse or ice cream.

1 cup sugar
½ cup (1 stick) butter or
  margarine, melted
½ cup shortening
1 egg
1 tablespoon molasses
¼ cup milk

1½ cups flour
1 heaping teaspoon
  cinnamon
½ teaspoon baking soda
½ teaspoon salt
1¾ cups quick-cooking
  oatmeal

Preheat oven to 325°F. In a mixing bowl cream together the sugar, butter or margarine, and shortening. Beat until light and fluffy. Add the egg, molasses, and milk. Sift together the flour, cinnamon, baking soda, and salt and add to the mixture alternately with the oatmeal. Use about 1 teaspoon of dough for each cookie (the inn shapes them with the back of a teaspoon) and place them 2 inches apart on a greased baking sheet. (If the dough is hard to spread, add an extra tablespoon of milk.) Bake 10-15 minutes or until the entire cookie is golden brown.

Makes 6 dozen.

MIRROR LAKE INN
Lake Placid, New York

PEANUT BUTTER COOKIES

A traditional favorite that never goes out of style.

½ cup peanut butter
½ cup (1 stick) butter
½ cup granulated sugar
½ cup firmly packed
   brown sugar

½ teaspoon vanilla
1 egg
1½ cups flour
1 teaspoon baking powder
½ teaspoon salt

Preheat oven to 350°F. In a mixing bowl cream together the peanut butter and butter. Gradually beat in the sugars until smooth. Add the vanilla and egg, beating until light and fluffy. Sift together the flour, baking powder, and salt and add to the batter, mixing thoroughly. Form the dough into small balls, place 1½ inches apart on a greased baking sheet, and press each cookie with the flat tines of a fork that has been dipped in flour. Bake 10-12 minutes.   *Makes 5 dozen.*

THE HEDGES
Blue Mountain Lake, New York

"BUTTER" COOKIES
WITH MARGARINE

Crisp, sugary cookies with a strong almond flavor. The dough freezes well and makes an acceptable substitute for Chinese almond cookies. To make these cookies, form the dough into logs 2½ inches in diameter, slice ½ inch thick, brush with beaten egg yolk, and place a blanched whole almond in the middle of each. This dough also can be used with a cookie press.

2 cups (4 sticks) margarine
2 tablespoons shortening
2 cups sugar
2 egg yolks
4 to 4½ teaspoons almond extract

5 cups flour
1 teaspoon salt
1 egg white beaten with 1 teaspoon water (optional)

Preheat oven to 375°F. In a mixing bowl cream together the margarine, shortening, and sugar. Beat in the egg yolks and almond extract. Stir in the flour and salt. Roll the dough into logs 1½ to 2 inches in diameter. Chill dough to facilitate slicing. Slice ¼ inch thick and arrange 2 inches apart on a baking sheet. If desired, brush the tops with egg white. Bake 8-10 minutes.

Makes 10-12 dozen.

THE KREBS
Skaneateles, New York

BROWNIES

Cora Krebs, the restaurant's founder, developed this recipe. The kitchen has a handwritten copy printed in a cookbook published in 1915. She recommends cake flour, but all-purpose flour will work just as well.

½ cup (1 stick) butter
2 squares unsweetened
   chocolate
2 eggs
1 cup sugar

1 cup chopped walnuts
Dash of vanilla
Dash of salt
½ cup flour

Preheat oven to 350°F. In a small saucepan melt the butter and chocolate. Remove from the heat and beat in the eggs, one at a time. Stir in the sugar, walnuts, vanilla, and salt. When smooth, add the flour. Pour the batter into a greased 9-inch square pan and bake 20 minutes.

Makes sixteen 2½-inch brownies.

GREENVILLE ARMS
Greenville, New York

CARAMEL CHOCOLATE
WORKSHOP BROWNIES

These rich, chewy brownies are sure to be kid-pleasers. The caramel flavor is subtle; milk chocolate chips give the brownies less of a chocolate taste and allow the caramel flavor to come through.

1 bag (14 ounces)
caramels
⅔ cup evaporated milk
1 package (18½ ounces)
Swiss chocolate cake
mix

¾ cup butter, melted
1 cup semisweet chocolate
pieces
1 cup chopped walnuts

Preheat oven to 350°F. In the top of a double boiler combine the caramels and ⅓ cup of the evaporated milk. Cook over boiling water, stirring occasionally, until melted. Keep warm. Combine the cake mix, butter, and remaining ⅓ cup evaporated milk in a bowl. Beat with a mixer at medium speed for 2 minutes. Spread half the batter in a greased 13x9x2-inch baking pan. Bake 6 minutes. Let cool 2 minutes. Spread the caramel mixture carefully over the baked layer. Sprinkle with the chocolate pieces. Stir ½ cup of the walnuts into the remaining batter. Drop by spoonfuls over the caramel layer. Sprinkle with the remaining walnuts. Bake 18 minutes. Cool and cut into bars or squares. *Makes 2 dozen.*

FRUIT DESSERTS AND PUDDINGS

BUTTERNUT INN
Chaffee, New York

GRANDMA'S RICE PUDDING

An old-fashioned classic with an unusual twist: This version is made with cooked rice, inspiring a fine use for rice left over from a dinner.

4 eggs, beaten	2½ cups milk
1 cup sugar	1 cup cooked rice
1½ teaspoons vanilla	1 cup raisins
¼ teaspoon salt	Cinnamon to taste

Preheat oven to 400°F. In a medium bowl combine the beaten eggs, sugar, vanilla, salt, and milk. Beat until smooth. Stir in the cooked rice and raisins. Pour the mixture into a 2-quart casserole dish and sprinkle the top with cinnamon. Place the dish in a larger dish and add water to come halfway up the sides of the outer dish. Bake 1 hour or until a knife inserted in the middle comes out clean.   *Serves 8.*

HUDSON HOUSE
Cold Spring, New York

LEMON CLOUD

A very light dessert, perfect for a summer night. Adjust the amount of sugar as desired and serve garnished with sprigs of fresh mint.

4 eggs
Juice of 2 lemons
1 ½ teaspoons unflavored
   gelatin

1 cup sugar (or less to
   taste)
1 cup heavy cream
Whipped cream

Separate the eggs. Put the whites in a large bowl and set aside. Put the yolks in a medium saucepan. Add the lemon juice to the yolks and sprinkle in the gelatin. Add ½ cup of the sugar and mix well. Cook over low heat, stirring constantly, for several minutes, until the mixture is smooth and the gelatin and sugar are completely dissolved. Pour the mixture into a large bowl and cool in the refrigerator for several minutes. Do not let the mixture set. Whip the egg whites with the remaining ½ cup of sugar, adding the sugar gradually, until the whites form stiff peaks. Fold the whites carefully into the cooled yolk base. Whip the heavy cream until soft peaks form and fold into the mixture until it is evenly blended. Spoon into one large decorative bowl or individual glasses. Chill 2 hours. Serve garnished with additional whipped cream.

Serves 4.

THREE VILLAGE INN
Stony Brook, New York

APPLE CRISP

A sweet dessert with a rich apple taste and a delightful crust. Also good with ice cream.

10 medium apples, peeled and sliced
2 teaspoons cinnamon
2 teaspoons granulated sugar
1½ cups brown sugar

1 cup plus 2 tablespoons flour
6 tablespoons butter
6 tablespoons margarine
¼ teaspoon salt
Whipped cream

Preheat oven to 350°F. In a medium bowl combine the apple slices, 1½ teaspoons cinnamon, and granulated sugar and mix thoroughly. Spread in a lightly buttered 9x13-inch pan. In the same bowl combine the brown sugar, flour, butter, margarine, ½ teaspoon cinnamon, and salt. Blend with a pastry cutter or two knives until the ingredients are mixed but not too moist. Spread the crumbs evenly over the apple mixture and pat down. Bake 45 minutes or until the apples are thoroughly cooked. (If topping browns too fast, cover the pan with brown paper.) Serve warm, topped with whipped cream.

Serves 8-10.

CAPTAIN SCHOONMAKER'S
High Falls, New York

PEACH DELIGHT STREUSEL

A fine snack for coffee or tea and a great breakfast treat for the weekend.

1 pound bread dough (buy it or make your own)	¼ cup butter or margarine
1 can (28 ounces) peaches	Cinnamon
¼ cup Bisquick	Nutmeg
½ cup sugar	Coconut
	Chopped nuts

Preheat oven to 350°F. Grease an 11x15-inch baking sheet and work the bread dough evenly into all the corners, as if you were making a pizza. Drain the peaches and reserve the juice. Finely slice the peaches on top of the dough. In a separate bowl combine the Bisquick, sugar, butter or margarine, and cinnamon and nutmeg to taste. Work the mixture with your hands until crumbly. Sprinkle on top of the peaches. Generously sprinkle the crumb layer with coconut and chopped nuts. Splash 3 tablespoons of reserved peach juice over the top and bake 25-30 minutes. Serve warm.   *Serves 10-12.*

THE HULBERT HOUSE
Boonville, New York

BLUEBERRY BUCKLE

Here's an old-fashioned dessert this inn has been making for many years.

¼ cup butter	½ teaspoon salt
¾ cup sugar	½ cup milk
1 egg	2 cups blueberries, lightly
1¾ cups flour	dusted with flour
2 teaspoons baking	Crumb Topping (recipe
powder	follows)

Preheat oven to 350°F. In a mixing bowl cream together the butter and sugar and beat until fluffy. Add the egg and beat well. Sift together the flour, baking powder, and salt and add to the creamed mixture alternately with the milk. Stir until smooth. Fold in the blueberries. Pour the batter into a greased 9-inch square pan and sprinkle with topping. Bake 35 minutes or until done.   *Serves 8-10.*

CRUMB TOPPING

¼ cup butter	½ teaspoon cinnamon
½ cup sugar	
⅓ cup flour (or more as	
needed)	

Combine all the ingredients and mix until crumbly. Add more flour if the mixture seems sticky.

CAPTAIN SCHOONMAKER'S
High Falls, New York

BLUEBERRY STRUDEL

A rich blueberry filling encased in a delicate, golden pastry, surprisingly easy to make. Great hot or cold. The inn reports success making it with canned, drained blueberries, bananas, cherry pie filling (add almonds), apples and raisins, or apricots.

6 sheets (9x13 inches each) filo dough	Coconut
	Chopped walnuts
1 cup fresh blueberries	Honey
Cinnamon	Melted butter
Nutmeg	Powdered sugar
Mace	

Preheat oven to 350°F. On a baking sheet lay out 6 sheets of filo dough, one directly on top of the other. In the middle make a row of blueberries from end to end. Season to taste with cinnamon, nutmeg, and mace and sprinkle to taste with coconut and chopped walnuts. Drizzle generously with honey. Fold the dough up like a jellyroll to make a long cylinder. Pinch the ends and brush generously with melted butter. Bake 20-25 minutes. Remove carefully. Sprinkle with powdered sugar, slice, and serve. *Serves 6.*

THE BENN CONGER INN
Groton, New York

CHOCOLATE MOUSSE

This elegant dessert is deceptively easy to prepare. Except for whipping the cream, the entire recipe can be made in a food processor. It freezes well and is available simply by defrosting.

8 ounces semisweet
  chocolate
1 cup sugar
1 tablespoon loose instant
  coffee
½ cup boiling water
1 cup (2 sticks) unsalted
  butter, softened

4 eggs
2 tablespoons dark rum or
  brandy
1 cup heavy cream
Whipped cream

Chop the chocolate coarsely. In the bowl of a food processor combine the chocolate, sugar, and coffee and process until finely ground. With the machine running, add the boiling water and run until the mixture is completely liquid. Add the butter while the mixture is still warm and process until smooth. Add the eggs, one at a time, and the rum or brandy. Scrape the mixture into a container and chill 2 hours. When the chocolate is slightly thickened, whip the cream until it is firm but soft and fold into the chocolate with a spatula. Pour through a funnel into eight wine glasses. Chill thoroughly. Serve with a spoonful of whipped cream on top. *Serves 8.*

TAVERN ON THE GREEN
New York, New York

TAVERN CHOCOLATE MOUSSE

Serve in glass dishes or in chocolate cups, garnished with a small dollop of whipped cream. If commercially made cups are not available, make your own: Melt 12-16 ounces semi-sweet or milk chocolate in a double boiler over simmering water. When the chocolate is melted, use a pastry brush to coat the insides of foil muffin cups. Place the coated cups in a muffin pan and freeze 5-10 minutes. Remove the cups one at a time from the freezer, peel off the foil, and refrigerate until ready to use.

4 egg whites
1 cup sugar
8 ounces semisweet
  chocolate, melted and
  cooled to lukewarm

1 pint (2 cups) heavy
  cream, whipped

In a medium bowl combine the egg whites and sugar. Beat together over a double boiler until very hot. Remove from heat and continue beating until the mixture is cool. Combine the melted chocolate and egg mixture and mix together well. Fold in the whipped cream. Spoon into serving dishes or chill and pipe into chocolate cups.
Serves 8-10.

THE ALGONQUIN
New York, New York

VICAR'S FOLLY

Andrew Anspach, managing director of this famed big-city inn, has denied that this dessert is simply a way for his talented literary guests to sneak a drink past their agents. It's simply a dessert that tastes good, he replies, and the sauce just happens to contain gin. Call it a lemon mousse.

8 eggs, separated	2 tablespoons grated
1¾ cups sugar	lemon peel
1 envelope unflavored	2 crushed macaroons
gelatin	Fruit Sauce (recipe
1 tablespoon water	follows)
6 tablespoons lemon juice	

In the top of a double boiler or in a pan over hot water beat the egg yolks and 1 cup of the sugar until the mixture thickens. Soften the gelatin in the water and blend into the hot mixture. Chill until partially set. In a large bowl beat the egg whites until they are slightly stiff but not dry. Gently fold in the remaining sugar and the lemon juice. Carefully fold the egg yolk, sugar, and gelatin mixture into the beaten egg whites. Pour the mixture into a 2-quart glass bowl and sprinkle with the grated lemon peel and crushed macaroons. Chill at least 2 hours. Serve with Fruit Sauce on the side.   *Serves 4-5.*

FRUIT SAUCE

1 tablespoon cornstarch
dissolved in 2
tablespoons water
1 cup pitted Queen Anne
cherries

1 cup cranberries
1 ½ tablespoons lemon
juice
½ cup gin

In the top of a double boiler combine the cornstarch, cherries, cranberries, and lemon juice and cook over hot water until the mixture is thick and clear. Remove from the heat and add the gin. Chill.

GENESEE FALLS INN
Portageville, New York

FROZEN RASPBERRY CREME

A cool, tangy-sweet, beautiful pastel pink dessert, just the thing to serve at the height of raspberry season.

1 pint sour cream
2 teaspoons vanilla
1 ½ cups sugar

1 pint fresh raspberries or
1 package (10 ounces)
frozen

In a mixing bowl combine the sour cream, vanilla, and sugar. Add the raspberries and blend well. Pour the mixture into individual 3- to 4-ounce molds or one large 1½-quart mold. Freeze. To serve, run the mold(s) under warm water, upend, and tap gently to loosen the frozen mixture. Arrange on a dessert plate.   *Serves 8.*

TAVERN ON THE GREEN
New York, New York

CHEF DIETER'S CRÈME BRULÉE

Subtly rich and smooth, this might head the list of your favorite desserts.

1 quart (4 cups) heavy cream	⅔ cup granulated sugar
1 vanilla bean	8 egg yolks
Pinch of salt	¼ cup brown sugar

Preheat oven to 300°F. In a heavy saucepan warm the cream. Add the vanilla bean and salt. In a medium bowl combine the granulated sugar and egg yolks. Beat well. Add the warmed cream and mix well. Pour the mixture into a 3-quart casserole or mold. Place the mold in a pan of hot water and bake 30 minutes. Cool 30 minutes. Sift the brown sugar over the top. Broil to form a glaze.

Serves 6.

THE BENN CONGER INN
Groton, New York

CRÈME BRULÉE

A lighter version of this classic dessert.

4 egg yolks
⅓ cup sugar
1 teaspoon vanilla
1 tablespoon dark rum

¼ cup milk
1¼ cups heavy cream
Brown sugar

Preheat oven to 350°F. Combine all the ingredients except the brown sugar in a mixing bowl. Blend well. Pour the mixture into four 5-ounce custard cups or small bowls and place the filled bowls in a pan of hot water. Bake 1¼ hours or until set. Chill. To serve, sprinkle a thin layer of brown sugar over the top and broil for a few minutes, until glazed.   *Serves 4.*

DEPUY CANAL HOUSE
High Falls, New York

FENNEL SORBET

An interesting use for fennel and a dessert your guests probably won't have tried before. Make sure to blend the ingredients until very smooth.

2 cups water	2 envelopes unflavored
2 bulbs fresh fennel	gelatin
1 ¼ cups sugar	1 cup heavy cream
¾ cup light corn syrup	½ cup ouzo or anisette

In a large, heavy saucepan combine the water and fennel bulbs and boil until the fennel is tender. Add the sugar and corn syrup and set aside. In a small bowl combine the gelatin and heavy cream and let sit until the gelatin dissolves. Stir the ouzo or anisette into the cream and gelatin and place in a blender along with the fennel and water. Blend until very smooth. Pour the mixture into a 9x12-inch shallow baking dish and freeze. Spoon the mixture into glass bowls and serve. *Serves 6.*

DIRECTORY OF NEW YORK STATE INNS

(The numbers in parentheses after the inns' names refer to the pages on which their recipes may be found.)

The Algonquin
(198, 199, 296)
59 West Forty-Fourth Street
New York, NY 10036
(212) 840-6800

The Athenaeum
(41, 44, 109, 129, 159, 282)
Chautauqua, NY 14722
(716) 357-4444

Asa Ransom House
(73, 121, 176, 254)
10529 Main Street
Clarence, NY 14031
(716) 759-2315

Auberge des 4 Saisons
(80, 84, 96, 168, 196, 206)
Route 42
Shandaken, NY 12480
(914) 688-2223

The Astoria
(26)
25 Main Street
Rosendale, NY 12472
(914) 658-8201

The Bakers
(14, 21, 24, 32, 35, 67, 229, 230)
Box 80
Stone Ridge, NY 12484
(914) 687-9795

The Bark Eater
(62)
Alstead Mill Road
Keene, NY 12942
(518) 576-2221

Bayberry Inn
(60, 75, 276)
County Road 39A
Southampton, NY 11968
(516) 283-4220

The Bird & Bottle Inn
(103, 114)
Old Albany Post Road
Garrison, NY 10524
(914) 424-3000

Bear Mountain Inn
(258)
Bear Mountain, NY 10911
(914) 786-2731

The Butternut Inn
(19, 77, 139, 224, 270, 288)
Route 16 and Genesee Road
Chaffee, NY 14030
(716) 496-8987

Beekman Arms
(137, 138, 208)
Rhinebeck, NY 12572
(914) 876-7077

Captain Schoonmaker's
(43, 291, 293)
Route 213
High Falls, NY 12440
(914) 687-7946

The Benn Conger Inn
(61, 294, 299)
206 West Cortland Street
Groton, NY 13073
(607) 898-5817

Le Chambord
(88, 92, 169, 192)
Route 52 and Carpenter Road
Hopewell Junction, NY 12533
(914) 221-1941

Big Moose Inn
(66, 185, 189, 216, 264)
Eagle Bay, NY 13331
(315) 357-2042

Colgate Inn
(127, 131, 183)
On the Green
Hamilton, NY 13346
(315) 824-2300

The Concord
(38, 39, 156, 202)
Kiamesha Lake, NY 12751
(914) 794-4000

Country Road Lodge
(37, 106, 184, 273)
Hickory Hill Road
Warrensburg, NY 12885
(518) 623-2207

DeBruce Country Inn
(152, 178)
DeBruce, NY 12758
(914) 439-3900

DePuy Canal House
(86, 120, 122, 220, 236, 240, 242,
260, 300)
Route 213
High Falls, NY 12440
(914) 687-7700

Garnet Hill
(54, 280)
North River, NY 12856
(518) 251-2821

Genesee Country Inn
(12, 23, 29, 58, 82, 281)
948 George Street
Mumford, NY 14511
(716) 538-2500

Genesee Falls Inn
(118, 191, 297)
Portageville, NY 14536
(716) 493-2484

Geneva on the Lake
(148, 205, 226)
1001 Lochland Road
Geneva, NY 14456
(315) 789-7190

The Gideon Putnam
(102, 108, 136, 170, 187)
Saratoga Springs, NY 12866
(518) 584-3000

Glen Iris Inn
(105, 144)
Letchworth State Park
Castile, NY 14427
(716) 493-2622

Gold Mountain Chalet
(195, 228)
P.O. Box 456
Spring Glen, NY 12483
(914) 647-4332

Greenville Arms
(56, 71, 146, 256, 262, 287)
Greenville, NY 12083
(518) 966-5219

Hansen's Adirondack Lodge
(53, 57, 74)
South Shore Road
Lake Pleasant, NY 12108
(518) 548-3697

The Hedges
(64, 271, 274, 283, 285)
Blue Mountain Lake, NY 12812
(518) 352-7325

The Horned Dorset Inn
(113, 210)
Leonardsville, NY 13364
(315) 855-7898

Hudson House
(180, 194, 222, 233, 246, 289)
2 Main Street
Cold Spring, NY 10516
(914) 265-9355

Huff House
(81, 128, 133, 275)
Roscoe, New York
(607) 498-9953
(914) 482-4579

The Hulbert House
(63, 111, 115, 261, 292)
Boonville, NY 13309
(315) 942-4318

The Inn at Cooperstown
(65)
16 Chestnut Street
Cooperstown, NY 13326
(607) 547-5756

Kittle House
(90, 119, 164, 182, 215, 247)
Route 117
Mt. Kisco, NY 10549
(914) 666-8044

The Krebs
(265, 286)
West Genesee Street
Skaneateles, NY 13152
(315) 685-5714

Millhof Inn
(18)
Route 43
Stephentown, NY 12168
(518) 733-5606

Lanza's Country Inn
(13, 50, 124, 132, 212)
R.D.2
Livingston Manor, NY 12758
(914) 439-5070

Mirror Lake Inn
(17, 45, 83, 104, 223, 232, 249, 284)
Lake Placid, NY 12946
(518) 523-2544

Lincklaen House
(42)
Cazenovia, NY 13035
(315) 655-3461

Mohonk Mountain House
(158, 227, 237)
New Paltz, NY 12561
(914) 255-1000
(212) 233-2244

The Mandana Inn
(181, 250)
1937 West Lake Road
Skaneateles, NY 13152
(315) 685-7798

Old Drovers Inn
(46, 112, 257)
Dover Plains, NY 13522
(914) 832-9311

The Merrill MaGee House
(40, 235)
2 Hudson Street
Warrensburg, NY 12885
(518) 623-2449

The Old Dutch Inn
(217, 231, 255)
Kinderhook, NY 12106
(518) 758-1676

The Otesaga and Cooper Inn
(204)
P.O. Box 311
Cooperstown, NY 13326
(607) 547-9931

Partridge Berry Inn
(193, 266)
Black River Road
Watertown, NY 13601
(315) 788-4610

Pleasant View Lodge
(140, 150, 200)
Freehold, NY 12431
(518) 634-2523

The Point
(76, 98, 116, 175, 268)
Saranac Lake, NY 12983
(518) 891-5674

The Redcoat's Return
(252)
Dale Lane
Elka Park, NY 12427
(518) 589-9858
(518) 589-6379

Rose Inn
(20, 91)
813 Auburn Road
Ithaca, NY 14851
(607) 533-4202

Roundup Ranch
(33, 126, 130, 165, 186, 248, 277)
Wilson Hollow Road
Downsville, NY 13755
(607) 363-7300

The 1770 House
(30, 34, 68, 70, 94, 117, 123, 171, 234, 241, 278)
143 Main Street
East Hampton, NY 11937
(516) 324-1770

Ship Lantern Inn
(93, 142)
Milton, NY 12547
(914) 795-5400
(914) 795-5407

Snapper Inn
(157, 161, 162, 177, 188, 190)
500 Shore Drive
Oakdale, NY 11769
(516) 589-0248

Springside Inn
(272)
Route 38 South
Auburn, NY 13021
(315) 252-7249

Tavern on the Green
(134, 218, 295, 298)
Central Park
at West 67th Street
New York, NY 10023
(212) 873-3200

Three Village Inn
(52, 110, 290)
150 Main Street
Stony Brook, NY 11790
(516) 751-0555

Troutbeck
(99, 151, 166, 214)
Leedsville Road
Amenia, NY 12501
(914) 373-9681

Tryon Inn
(160, 174, 251)
124 Main Street
Cherry Valley, NY 13320
(607) 264-9301

Ujjala's
(16, 36, 72)
2 Forest Glen
New Paltz, NY 12561
(914) 255-6360

Union Hall Inn
(69, 107, 238)
2 Union Place
Johnstown, NY 12095
(518) 762-3210

The William Seward Inn
(15, 22)
South Portage Road
Westfield, NY 14784
(716) 326-4151

Winter Clove Inn
(55, 78, 154, 239, 259)
Round Top, NY 12473
(518) 622-3267

Ye Hare 'n Hounds Inn
(213)
64 Lakeside Drive
Bemus Point, NY 14712
(716) 386-2181

INDEX